Lyrics for the Adults

A Critical Examination of N.W.A.'s
Straight Outta Compton

Featuring Exclusive Interviews

Edited by K.B. Daniels

Sideshow Media Group Press
Los Angeles / Austin

SIDESHOW MEDIA GROUP
Los Angeles / Austin
www.sideshowmediagroup.com

Special Thanks: Eric Poppelton, Kevin Hosmann, The D.O.C., Bob Sanford, Josh Bucher, Dan Gentile

© 2014 by SSMG Press
All Rights Reserved

ISBN 978-0-9761465-5-1

FIRST EDITION

10 9 8 7 6 5 4 3 2 1

Manufactured in the United States of America

Contents

Introduction	11

PART I: The Music

Straight Outta Compton	17
Fuck tha Police	25
Gangsta Gangsta	31
If it Ain't Ruff	35
Parental Discretion is Advized	43
8 Ball (Remix)	47
Something Like That	53
Express Yourself	59
Compton's In tha House	65
I Ain't tha One	71
Something 2 Dance 2	77

PART II: The Interviews

Interview with Eric Poppelton	85
Interview with Kevin Hosmann	99
Interview with The D.O.C.	135

Lyrics for the Adults

Introduction

Straight Outta Compton may be the greatest hip hop album of all time. It's at least in the conversation. Not because every track is flawless or each verse rises above the previous one, but because its anthems became cultural touchstones, and the album taps deeply into that ever-elusive set of "universal themes" that allow the listener to practically assume the identity of the speaker. With the release of *Straight Outta Compton* in 1988, N.W.A. established the gangster-criminal dynamic that still rules hardcore rap.

Straight Outta Compton is a product of South Central Los Angeles in 1988. The most successful commercial rap albums of 1986 and 1987 were iconic: Run-D.M.C.'s *Raising Hell*, the Beastie Boys' *License to Ill* (the first rap album to top the Billboard charts), and LL Cool J's *Bigger and Deffer*. However, none of them would portend the violent explosion of gangsta rap ignited by N.W.A. and *Straight Outta Compton*. Neither Run-D.M.C. nor the Beastie Boys nor LL Cool J had adopted the persona of a drug-dealing murderer. As The D.O.C. says later in this volume, rap music has never recovered from this trope of

"Everyone out there is still a dope dealer who will kill you." A possible exception to the mid-80s trend of "safe" rap was Public Enemy's successful 1988 release of *It Takes a Nation of Millions to Hold Us Back*. Yet, Run-D.M.C., the Beastie Boys, LL Cool J, and Public Enemy were all New York acts—N.W.A. was the first prominent West coast group to emerge in the hip hop world.

Still, their murderous image was one carefully crafted. Eazy-E was the driving force behind establishing this street credibility as he was, in fact, selling marijuana and affiliated with the Bloods gang. However, Eazy realized he could potentially earn more from capitalizing on the mass (read *white*) interest in LA street life. So, with Jerry Heller, he started Ruthless Records.

The first image of N.W.A. most people saw was on the cover of a cassette tape: six young, black men, one of them pointing a gun at the camera, a black background, a graffiti script, and a "Parental Advisory: Explicit Content" sticker. In this book we talk with the photographer and art director who created that image.

This book seeks to dig deeper into each track of the album, to examine what specifically happened over the course of the track—and the album's progression. We try to understand why the lyrics worked so perfectly, how the beats were put together, and what the album meant to a generation of listeners.

The analysis of the music is followed by extensive new interviews with Eric Poppelton, who photographed N.W.A and Kevin Hosmann, who designed the album cover of *Straight Outta Compton*. The book closes with an exclusive interview with influential rap legend The D.O.C., who appeared on several tracks and served as an integral writing partner of N.W.A. during the production of *Straight Outta Compton*.

Lyrics for the Adults

Part I
The Music

Lyrics for the Adults

Straight Outta Compton

Opening with an *a cappella* declaration from Eazy-E that, "You are now about to witness the strength of street knowledge," a souped-up sample of James Brown's "Funky Drummer" commences, accented by a "yeah" and an "ohhh" that would later inspire a more familiar interpolation used in the pop hit "It takes Two" by Rob Base and DJ EZ-Rock.

Ice Cube was, at this point, the group's strongest lyricist, and usually the lead-off batter. This formula was still being worked out in the various N.W.A. musical efforts, including "N.W.A. and the Posse" (a posse which would later outnumber N.W.A. when members of the Fila Fresh Crew, Ron De Vu and The Arabian Prince were finally tallied), as well as what some purists consider N.W.A.'s first full-length release, *Eazy-Duz-It*, an album credited to Eazy-E, but one for which he only provided some lead vocals. All production, lyrics and many of the accompanying verses were supplied by members of N.W.A.

Using the most common journalistic formula (Who? What? When? Where? Why? and How?), Cube gives us the answers, "Straight Outta Compton, crazy motherfucker named Ice Cube. From the gang called Niggas with Attitudes. When I'm called off, I got a sawed off. Squeeze the trigger and bodies are hauled off."

It is important to recognize that until this point, N.W.A records had largely been semi-journalistic, where members of the group took a third-party approach to reporting about the life they saw on the streets. "Dopeman" is a prime example. However, with *Straight Outta Compton*, and some would argue on *Eazy-Duz-It*, members of the group became characters in the drama they reported on, acting and speaking in the first person. In *Straight Outta Compton*, Cube claims to have a "crime record like Charles Manson." Ironically, music produced during this period is likely the only form of art where it was assumed the artist had lived everything that they sang (or rapped) about. Rock band Guns N Roses ran into similar issues around the same time. N.W.A.'s listeners, for the most part, believed that the group had killed many opponents, had thousands of sexual exploits, and generally lived a gangster's fantasy. Most listeners would have been surprised to learn that Ice Cube had actually just returned from architecture school in Arizona when the record was recorded. It should be noted that none of the members of N.W.A. were ever convict-

Lyrics for the Adults

ed of a violent crime. In fact, when charges of battery were leveled at member, Dr. Dre, (charges that were later settled out of court) it almost ruined his career in the music business.

While the lyrics were shocking and hard-hitting because of the profanity and violence, they were somewhat less than poetic in many places. Members of the group often had trouble finding words that rhymed with Compton, their California hometown, which not only appears in several of the songs but in the album title as well. "Stompin'" was used *ad nauseaum* to complete verses.

"Niggas start to mumble. They wanna rumble. Mix 'em up and cook 'em in a pot like gumbo," continues Cube, again showing his flair as the senior lyricist of the group. As Cube concludes, it is interesting to note that in keeping with Dre's production style, the title of the song is never mentioned in the chorus. Neither is there any chant or words spoken by a lyricist, only samples and scratches further exploring the subject matter of the song. This chorus style first soared to popularity on N.W.A.'s first hit, "Boyz in da Hood," on Eazy's *Eazy-Duz-It*. Also popular with Dre, is speaking to the lyricist in the vocal booth from the mixing board over the single channel mic. This method transitions us from the chorus of the song to MC Ren's verse with Dre instructing, "Yo Ren! (What's up?) Tell 'em where you from!"

Ren reinforces his role as the second-mate lyricist, a title he would never shake and that would later stifle his attempted solo career, responding that he is ANOTHER crazy ass nigga and not THE crazy ass nigga of the group. Ren's frustration with his position seems to often come out in subtle ways in many N.W.A. verses. He states here, "I'm a bad motherfucker and you know this! But the pussy ass niggas won't show this," inferring that it is the fault of opposing forces he has not found his own recognition. Ren does continue to reinforce key N.W.A. ideals in his verse stating, "I don't give a fuck, I'm gonna make my snaps, if not from the records from jackin' or craps."

Statements such as this would go on to convince their audience that the members of N.W.A. had only taken a vacation from crime long enough to do a record and if that didn't show success, they would be back to their old ways in no time. Ironically, when their music experienced massive success, they decidedly reported to the audience that they had returned to their old ways anyway. Future records almost solely concentrated on the fact that they were murders and criminals of every caliber with an uncontrollable urge for sex.

Towards the end of his verse, Ren insists that he is not a "right hand" but the hand its self. However, the listener easily recognizes that this is just not true. Many in N.W.A.'s audience did appreciate Ren's bravado in making such statements, usually those who felt somewhat like "right hands" themselves in real life. The phenomenon of mentioning which member of the group was your favorite often revealed a lot about a person, and more importantly what type person they were on the hip hop landscape. This was not at all unlike members of the Beatles audience worshipping the member of the group they were most likely to match in a personality test.

Most baffling in Ren's contribution to the album's opening are the lyrics, "Security is maximum and that's a law, R-E-N spells Ren but I'm raw." One is left to ponder if the security is for the audience or for Ren and just why it is law. The comparison of REN somehow being related to RAW is also confusing, other than the fact that they both begin with an R and are three letters long.

Eazy-E rounds out the lineup on "Straight Outta…" with another introduction from Dre stating that Eazy is his name and the boy is coming straight outta Compton. On Eazy's solo album, the many contributors helped construct an interesting character who was occasionally self-deprecating, reluctant to reveal his advanced age, and as much of a prankster as he was a gangster. It is unclear if Eazy or some other member of the group decided his image needed to be beefed up a bit, but this is exactly what happened. It is on this album and specifically this song that Eazy begins selling himself as mentally ill. This was a bit trendy at the time in the emerging world of gangster rap, as Houston's Geto Boys had taken the idea to an extreme claiming to be mentally ill rapists who enjoyed necrophilia. Eazy would go on to later announce that his next solo effort would be titled "Temporary Insanity." This album never came to fruition, though Eazy did make many concert appearances and photo shoots wearing a straight jacket.

Eazy announces this transition in his persona by stating he is a brother who would smother your mother and make your sister think he loves her. He goes on to make a statement that also becomes a standard of the N.W.A. philosophical playbook: that he doesn't give a fuck. This attitude of claiming not to care about anyone or anything goes on to develop as the central theme of gangsta rap, with the slight footnote of money's value. Real gangsters would go on to claim that nothing was worth caring about except money. Ironically, this was a sentiment shared by much of conservative corporate Reagan/Bush-Era America, we would later find out. As a matter of fact, Eazy would later find so much in common with conservative lawmakers and corporations that a donation to the Republican party ended up earning him a dinner invitation to the White House with the President as a guest of honor. Accepting the invitation would later come back to haunt his reputation on the streets and cause him to be ridiculed on records by Ice Cube, who would claim, "I'd never have dinner with the President!"

Musically, "Straight Outta Compton" borrows it's beat from from "Funky Drummer" by James Brown, which Dre would also use as the base for the album's next song, "Fuck tha Police." "You'll Like It Too" by Funkadelic, "Get Me Back on Time, Engine No. 9" by Wilson Pickett, "Amen, Brother" by The Winstons, "West Coast Poplock" by Ronnie Hudson and the Street People and "One for the Treble" by Davy DMX also lent elements to the cut.

The song comes to a close with Dre declaring, "Damn that shit was dope!" It is worth noting that since the album was released in the area when cassette tapes and records ruled the shelves, the end of "Straight Outta Compton" seems to immediately flow into "Fuck the Police," with nothing but a scratch separating the two cuts. Listeners rarely stopped the music between the two records and often referred to them in tandem.

"Straight Outta Compton" demonstrated a fury, an intensity and articulation not seen on any previous efforts by the group. It was clear that they had stepped up their game. Even the music was faster paced and more intense than anything Dre had served up previously. The song sets the tone of the album and serves as one of the great "Side One-Track One's" of all time. The rest of the album goes on to demonstrate more skill from N.W.A. However, this author would suggest that we learn nothing further about the band after the first song. The rest of the album seems to unpack and reinforce the ideas put out in "Straight Outta..." Even the album's most revered cut, "Fuck the Police" takes its thematic cues out of lyrics and vibes established in this lead cut. Perhaps part of the genius of this is its simplicity. The lead song, the album title and the ideas that serve as the album's thesis are all summed up in those three words—Straight Outta Compton.

—JKB

Lyrics for the Adults

Fuck tha Police

Straight Outta Compton's most celebrated track was the result of an incident with a paintball gun—according to Dr. Dre. As Dre has related the story in the press, he and Eazy-E were riding around town and using Eazy's paintball gun to fire at people waiting for the bus. The police pulled over Eazy and Dre, drew their guns, and had the rappers lay face down on the street while they dealt with the situation. Supposedly, Eazy and Dre went directly to the studio and recorded the anthem that would eventually become #417 on *Rolling Stone*'s list of the 500 greatest songs of all time. Interestingly enough, the song was never released or promoted as a single—all acclaim and publicity was strictly word of mouth.

The song begins with the voice of The D.O.C, an artist from the Fila Fresh Crew, whom Dr. Dre was developing as a solo act. The D.O.C., speaking as a faux bailiff, announces that N.W.A. court is in full effect and that Judge Dre will be presiding. One must assume that is why Dre does not rap on the record, as he is busy with his judicial duties. The members of N.W.A. are then introduced as prosecuting attorneys in the case of N.W.A. versus the police department. One has to wonder how the police will ever get a fair shake in N.W.A. court if the case is N.W.A. versus the police department. However, this references the inability of N.W.A. to ever get a fair trial in a public court room versus a police department. The D.O.C. completes his swearing in by asking the prosecuting attorneys (as opposed to the witnesses) to tell the truth, the whole truth, and nothing but the truth so help their black asses.

Again, Ice Cube is called upon to lead things off for the lyrical team. He launches into what is some of the most quoted material from the song. "Fuck the police, coming straight from the underground, young nigga got it bad cause I'm brown." Cube goes immediately for the jugular and ups the charges against the police from overplaying the paintball gun charges directly to murder. He states "police think they have the authority to kill a minority." It is where Cube goes next that affirms the group's then-recent metamorphosis from street reporters to characters in their own tale. It is also the lyrical direction that would bring threats from the F.B.I., as well as a refusal on the part of many in law enforcement to patrol N.W.A.'s concerts. Cube claims he will "beat a police out of shape and when I'm finished, bring the yellow tape to tape off the scene of the slaughter"—foretelling a "bloodbath of cops dying in L.A." Cube suggests that black police officers are bigger offenders than white officers, stating that "black police (are) showing out for the white cop." This single line would inspire a key scene in John Singleton's film *Boyz N da Hood* as well as countless other mentions in film, television, and music.

Dre uses a faux-scratched sample of Eazy-E saying "fuck the police" on the chorus, which was a rarity at that time for a producer. The title to Dre's songs did not make it's way into the chorus for the most part, a dynamic which set N.W.A. apart from most of their counterparts at that time.

Again, Ren is called in for lyrical backup on the second verse. Cube's statements are basically reinforced with several additional threats to kill any policeman who gives the emcee trouble. Eazy-E adds a few statements of interest claiming when police view his ID, his "identity by its self causes violence." E also claims that without a gun and a badge, police are suckers "in a uniform waiting to get shot."

Musically, the song is one of the more complex pieces on the album, utilizing elements of "Funky President" and "Funky Drummer" by James Brown to create the beat. Elements from "It's My Thing" by Marva Whitney, "Boogie Back" by Roy Ayers, "Feel Good" by Fancy, and "Be Thankful for What

You Got" by William DeVaughn are used to create the rest of the musical background and chorus. Dre also sampled work he produced on Eazy-E's "Ruthless Villain" on the cut.

The cut winds down with "Judge Dre" taking a break from his doctoral practice to read the verdict that the jury has found the police department guilty of being a "redneck, whitebread, chickenshit muthafucka." A stereotypical white voice, assumedly representing the police department, begs the contrary as the track fades into history.

Though the cut was not the first in popular music to challenge the police, nor even the first in rap, it remains the standard by which all other anti-authority songs are measured in hip hop—if not modern music. Some critics have compared Ice Cube's venture into family friendly film the equivalent of anti-establishment hippies of the 1960s buying mini-vans and starting multi-million-dollar software firms in Silicon Valley. Though many hip hop artists since have created music that realistically paint pictures of life on the street and the evils of law enforcement, all seem but bricks on the foundations that N.W.A. laid with "Fuck tha Police."

Socially, the song seemed to angrily demand attention to an unjust element of society that many claimed was overexerted or just did not exist. It took

Lyrics for the Adults

time for N.W.A.'s claims to be verified. But since the release of the song, it has become pop culture common knowledge that the Los Angeles Police Department has not always fairly served and protected. Even though the group was specifically targeting law enforcement in their own neighborhoods and backyards, the sentiment struck a nerve around the country where many minorities would relate and echo similar experiences and treatment. This outrage would even spill to the extremes of society in pop culture staples such as the films of Kevin Smith. Smith's recurring character Jay would often cite and recite "Fuck tha Police" as an anthem rallying against those who opposed his drug dealing ways.

Famously, the F.B.I. and U.S. Secret Service caught wind of the song and sent a letter to Ruthless Records stating their displeasure with the message of the song—historic precedent that has yet to be repeated in the music business. Additionally, several rock bands covered the song in the coming years and the tune would be come a classic American protest song, no doubt in part because of the L.A. Riots, which turned out to make the song prophetic.

—JKB

Lyrics for the Adults

Gangsta Gangsta

If there is any track on the album that completely confirms for the listener that *Straight Outta Compton* is a work of fiction and not documentary, it is "Gangsta Gangsta." Few, if any, listeners may have consciously noted this, but the fictional framework is laid down in the spoken intro (by an apparently Hispanic gangster/victim) and the first few lines of the lyrics:

> *Here's a little somthin bout a nigga like me*
> *Never should've been let out the penitentiary.*
> *Ice Cube would like to say*
> *That I'm a crazy muthafucker from around the way*
> *Since I was a youth, I smoke weed out*

The fact that Ice Cube so smoothly rhymes "nigga like me" with the five-syllabled "penitentiary" allows the listener to ignore the bravado. While "Ice Cube" is a recently released felon with long history of drug abuse and murder, the author, O'Shea Jackson, was a 19-year old who'd recently been let out the Phoenix Institute of Technology architectural drafting program. The nerd aesthetic clearly did not (yet) have the potential for hip-hop immortality that smoking weed as a 12-year-old murderer did. From a business standpoint, assuming a gangster persona undoubtedly made the most economic sense.

Ice Cube showcases some of his finest rhyming ability in this track and has no problem pushing the limits of what might be considered acceptable or even ethical behavior for a gangster. "Takin' a life or two, that's what the hell I do."

Also rare for songs on this album, "Gangsta Gangsta" has a traditional verse-chorus structure. The first verse contains one of the most famous lines in rap: "Life ain't nothin' but bitches and money." This sentiment succinctly sums up the dreamlife that Ice Cube and N.W.A. were trying to conjure with all of *Straight Outta Compton* (along with a profound dislike of the corrupt LAPD).

The N.W.A. of "Gangsta Gangsta" is not content to sit back and wait for danger to come to them or casually defend their civil rights. As Ren says in the second verse, "Let's start some shit." The gangster's gangster is not shy about attacking those on his shitlist, and has no problem using a shotgun at close range: "Boom boom boom."

The track amazingly mentions almost all of N.W.A.'s obsessions: Daytons (rims), "bitches in biker shorts", 8 Ball (Olde English 800 malt liquor), '64 Impalas, the police, weed. The song was also instrumental in establishing Compton as a mythical place that could harbor (and give life to) the most villainous killers on the planet. Compton is Juarez, Somalia, Scarface, and Stalingrad all rolled into one.

There is a popular Internet meme that juxtaposes an image of Ice Cube holding an AK-47 and an image of Cube the actor sitting in a canoe, wearing a lifejacket, holding the paddle at about the same angle as the AK. This juxtaposition sums up how far Ice Cube has moved away from the mythical gangster life and into mainstream popular culture, but it also points up how illusory, and how easily, an image (be it Hollywood or Gangsta Rap) can be constructed and rebuilt.

A number of other acts released covers or tracks titled "Gangsta Gangsta" but most notable was C-Murder and Snoop Dogg's version of the song for the 20th Anniversary Edition of *Straight Outta Compton*.

—MBB

Lyrics for the Adults

If It Ain't Ruff

by Dan Gentile

Straight Outta Compton is like a car crash you pass on the road except instead of the curiosity and voyeurism of disaster drawing you in, MC Ren is screaming at you to pay attention to him but that if you pay the wrong kind of attention he's going to shoot you. So you better just nod your head, wave your hands from side to side, and enjoy yourself. You don't really have any other choice in the matter.

On "If It Ain't Ruff" MC Ren is given his own shot at defining the image and aesthetics of the group. Rapping over alternating guitar samples from Average White Band's "A Star in the Ghetto", Ren asserts himself as a natural-born antagonist. He establishes an easy to loathe persona, that of a violent, fear-inducing, girlfriend-stealing hoodlum from Compton. The biographical truth behind this image is debatable, but it doesn't really affect the appeal of the song. In fact, using authenticity as a criterion for enjoying despicably violent entertainment is arguably despicable in itself. Whether Ren is or isn't a cold-hearted, shoot your mother for a dollar style killer, he's in a position to report on that type of figure. If one isn't blinded by the criminal nature of the content and chooses to accept N.W.A.'s lyrics as journalism and cultural commentary, the group's underdog status and charismatic bravado in the face of dismal context makes their success worth rooting for.

The sample source for the song has surprisingly parallel themes to N.W.A.'s back-story. A collaboration between Ben E. King and Average White Band, the lyrics of "A Star in the Ghetto" dismiss the signifiers traditionally associated with success in the music industry. The song shows disdain for the Grammy awards and Rock and Roll Hall of Fame, as well as established institutions such as Hollywood, Broadway, and Carnegie Hall. Since the song's creation Ben E. King and Average White Band have both been lauded with the very honors they refute in the song. Like N.W.A., these musicians step outside of their own personal experiences to convey sentiments that are easy to identify with. The message and attitude of the song applies more accurately to the then-ignored West Coast hip-hop scene that gave rise to N.W.A than the canonized blues musicians who wrote it.

Dr. Dre takes the introduction from "A Star in the Ghetto" and adds a few touches of his own. Average White Band's opening guitar line stinks of Gfunk, but in the original version it's quickly overshadowed by string and horn countermelodies. Dre ditches everything but the hard-hitting drum line and picked guitar figure. He adds a shaker to create an ominous pulsing groove and pans reverbed scratches to give the beat a large sense of space. After a brief instrumental intro, Ren jumps on the track and delivers an opening two lines that are perhaps his strongest in the song.

Threatening assertions and their reciprocal depictions of fear are Ren's lyrical bread and butter. In the song's first line he declares himself a villain and the listener a hostage forcefully captivated but repulsed by Ren's persona. His threatening nature is a source of control over the audience and they are unexpectedly hypnotized by his charisma. The hostage-taking scenario also explores the idea of surprise, one of N.W.A.'s primary themes. Nobody expected the west coast's ascendant rise in popularity and the group takes every opportunity to remind listeners that they're coming out of left field.

The second line extends the metaphor using the same cause and effect structure but integrates less traditionally antagonistic imagery. Ren continues the hostage-taking line of imagery by advising them to "cover their head" and hide on the ground like an ostrich. This is Ren at his sharpest lyrically, reappropriating otherwise tame images into extended metaphors declaring his powers of intimidation.

Other than frightening the listener, Ren's secondary goal is to denounce critics that question his authenticity. This begins in the third and fourth lines of the song as he describes the dichotomy created by his personal history. He directly addresses commentators who question the reality behind his image. His success is jealousy inducing to people who came from the same upbringing and question why Ren and his crew take it upon themselves to speak out. These critics eventually realize that the reason N.W.A. rose up above their peers is simply because they were cool enough to pull it off.

It's important that Ren establishes this idea of authenticity, despite the questionable foundation in fact, in order to give his message credibility. Part of the frustration that runs through the group's lyrics is based on the lack of commentary regarding their cultural position, and if they don't establish themselves as primary sources, the message loses its power because most listeners don't want to identify with a blatantly fabricated image. Although most fans can't relate to the Boyz in the Hood style violence that N.W.A. have famously become intertwined with, the listener can easily recognize the age-old theme of coming from nothing, a claim that the group defends throughout the album.

The song's chorus is the most blatant argument for Ren's authenticity, a simple reflexive boast that "if it ain't ruff, it ain't me." His identity is intertwined with the idea of appearing tougher than rocks. He denounces even the idea of being soft, the possibility doesn't exist. He isn't refined, cultured, or sophisticated, he's ruff. He takes the traditionally negative term and uses it as a stamp of pride, which is what N.W.A. is all about. Not bad meaning bad but bad meaning good. Taking pride in this lack of refinement is another method by which listeners can relate to Ren's image.

Not lyrically the strongest track on the album, Ren starts to sound like a bit of a broken record. He carries the same themes throughout, doing a passable job of depicting himself as someone you don't want to mess with, but he doesn't really break any new ground thematically. Several times throughout the song Ren awkwardly uses a reflexive lyrical conceit, essentially reusing the same phrase twice for no apparent reason but to complete a rhyme. It's distracting and proof that at this point in his career Ren simply isn't quite up to snuff lyrically with some of the other group members, but if you ignore the nonsensical repetition and occasionally disconnected statements, there are a few gems in the "ruff". (too much? i couldn't resist)

The most interesting lyrics are Ren's attempts to flip everyday imagery into signifiers of fear, intimidation, and charisma. "Get a cold rag and wipe your neck" is a simple line, but it's a commanding way for Ren to once again illustrate a punchy cause and effect. He's so in charge that he's going to make you sweat then condescendingly tell you to go fix the problem. In the next line he says that you might as well clean your face while you're at it to avoid acne, an awkwardly juvenile insult coming from a supposedly stone-cold killing machine and an indicator that he isn't nearly as skilled at crafting longer more complicated chains of lyrics.

The third verse features another good example of flipping an ordinary image. Referencing the do not disturb sign often found hanging from the handles of hotel doors, Ren lets you know he doesn't want to be bothered, and that usually when he doesn't want to be bothered it's because he's deciding who he wants to fuck with next. His default state is that of the antagonist.

But despite all of MC Ren's violent and aggressive tendencies, no one he directs his lyrics at can seem to deny his charisma. This love-hate relationship between Ren and his audience is representative of the whole idea behind gangsta rap and the reason an entire generation was genuinely dumbfounded by the genre's appeal. As N.W.A. broke into the mainstream, the majority of their listeners weren't urban youth who identified with the criminal personas created by the group, but rather suburban kids drawn in by familiar themes filtered through an inherently foreign cultural lens. Most fans may not be able to sympathize to the criminal elements of N.W.A., but they can no doubt relate to their greater myth of working towards one's goals from a culturally, geographically, and economically disadvantaged position.

Lyrics for the Adults

Parental Discretion iz Advised

PARENTAL DISCRETION IZ ADVISED at first seems to be a throwaway track—just a chance to get all the players a verse each on a simplistic track, but this usually formulaic approach ends up producing the most vertiginous assault of rhymes, segues, and stylized diction on the album. It turns out that these verses were meant to showcase each MC's talent on the mic (thusly, Arabian Prince, as a quasi-member of the group, is excluded from participating and Yella, who does not speak on the album, is relegated to just being mentioned, albeit prominently).

The first verse begins with a question indicating that this is indeed the last "record" on the album. Although the track was the last recorded, it does not appear last on either the CD, cassette, or vinyl. Remixes engineered late in the game were thrown on the album by Ruthless (read Heller) and stuck at the bottom of the track listing without input from the artists.

The first verse is saved for The D.O.C.—not a full-fledged member of the group, but at the time of the album, by far the most closely aligned (in terms of lyrical style and writing talent) non-member. It's not clear if the D.O.C. was ever paid for his work on *Straight Outta Compton* [he also portrays the narrator on "Fuck tha Police," but flubs the line "Judge Dre presiding" by saying "residing"]. He reminds us "upcoming is my album" and "listen to the single and you'll be like 'yo, I gotta get it." The circular structure of the verse begins and ends with a question for Dre.

Dre's verse repeats the theme of knowledge introduced in the prologue to the album ("Let knowledge be the tool"). Knowledge, as N.W.A. uses the term, is synonymous with black empowerment, a two-pronged approach that combines physical strength, aggression, and violence with the power of wisdom, information, and intellectual craftiness. Dre then proceeds to contradict himself by claiming "I don't give a fuck about a radio play." Maybe that's true, but then why allow tracks like "Express Yourself" and "Something 2 Dance 2"—sanitized, whitewashed pseudo-pop songs—on your album? Why not do an entire album hardcore and leave it at that? Dollars. Bank. Selling those albums at Wal-Mart means cleaning them up a bit to get them on the radio. And yet clearly Dre struggles with this contradiction, preemptively claiming he doesn't give a fuck before you can even label him a sellout. This tension will contribute to the group (and the success of their music) falling apart as quickly as it came together. A confusing lyric in this verse is Dre stating "Yo, it's Dre, so fuck the mind of Minolta." (All online lyric sites have transcribed something like "minor minalta"—and Dre's slight slurring and rushing of the line doesn't help lend clarity.) Those not up on their 1980s popular advertising history might not even be aware of the corporate slogan "Brought to you by the mind of Minolta." [Snoop Dogg later copies the lyric on his track "Serial Killer" {"Deep, deep, like the mind of Minolta."}]. The camera company was sold to Konica and later sold all of its camera business to Sony, but the ominous tagline, clearly voiced by an older white man, represented innovation, heterogeneous technology, and likely white-not-black knowledge and power. The line sticks out in the verse as bizarre and nearly nonsensical, Dre desperate to compose a meaningful rhyme, although he does follow it up later with the staccato "C-c-c-c-c-cameras are flashing" allusion.

Ren's verse contains several lyrics that stand out for their originality, but ultimately do not add up to the quality of Ice Cube's master performance (although Cube and Ren both over-rely on simple rhymes ending in "it").

"I be what is known as a bandit," begins the verse that towers over the others in terms of lyrical skill. Ice Cube's ability to craft lyrics and then deliver them in a hypnotic flowing style is on display here at it's finest and most emphatic. He even proclaims it: "What's next is the flex of a genius / My rap is stutter-steppin if you seen this."

Eazy-E begins his verse with acknowledging the audience's surprise that he would even be included amongst the rap-virtuoso performances of his colleagues: "Little did they know that I would be arrivin' / But it's surprisin', rockin' it from where I've been." (It's worth noting that the tendency to drop the terminal -*g* in speech, thought to be mostly a Southern affectation, is not so much regional as rural/urban and remains part of the casual hip-hop vernacular.) Eazy's verse, unlike those of his compatriots, focuses almost solely on his sexual prowess.

—MBB

Lyrics for the Adults

8 Ball (Remix)

There is a long-standing tradition in hip hop, where emcees proclaim loyalty to various brands that they believe define them and their style. The breakout moment for this trend was Run DMC's classic anthem, "My Adidas," where Darryl and Joe created a cultural phenomenon around shiny Adidas tracksuits and unlaced tennis shoes. The song directly led to hip hop's first great endorsement deal from a major company. No other musical genre has granted so much free advertising to the product industries, while determining the success and failure of brand based styles and trends.

While Ice Cube would later benefit monetarily by recording advertising spots for St. Ides malt liquor, when he and Eazy-E wrote 8 Ball, they really had no motivation to pay homage to their favorite beverage, other than pure love for Olde English 800, nicknamed in urban communities 8 Ball. This use of 8 Ball should not be confused with the same slang used in Anglo communities, referring to 3.5 grams of cocaine. "8 Ball" along with "Dopeman" first appeared on N.W.A.'s debut L.P., *N.W.A. and the*

Posse. Also, as with "Dopeman," only the beat is remixed for *Straight Outta Compton*, as the lyrics seem to remain virtually untouched.

*"I don't drink Brass Monkey,
like the beats funky,
nickname Eazy-E, yo, 8-Ball junkie"*

The opening lines of "8 Ball" are a response to another alcoholic ode that was released two years before, "Brass Monkey" by The Beastie Boys. There seems to be some disagreement among hip hop and alcohol enthusiasts about the exact recipe for a Brass Monkey. Some claim that the mix consists of vodka, dark rum and orange juice, with the dark rum giving the beverage it's brass-like color when mixed with the orange juice. Others argue the version of Brass Money more commonly found in more ethnic settings was actually malt liquor (usually Olde English 800) mixed with orange juice. Regardless of the ingredients, Eazy-E, did not drink it.

Eazy goes on to describe a scenario where he is driving to hang out with friends, with an unusually cold 40 oz. (the recommended dosage for any respectable hip hop head) of 8 Ball in his lap. He goes on to circumvent a policeman, drink while driving and listen to Marvin Gaye's *Greatest Hits*. E concludes the verse, getting distracted by a woman with a gifted rear end and butter face, by completing his inebriation while cruising through Compton, California. The chorus of the song is classic Dre for this era, using the words of other emcees and singers to tell his own story and make his unique contribution to the song.

True to the geographic appreciation that caused him to throw the name of his city in the title of this record, Eazy continues to provide GPS-like directions for his journey, telling us exactly which streets he is taking (Slauson towards Crenshaw) on his route through the second verse. Again, Mr. Wright is paused by the police, who he is afraid might take offense to his playing Marvin Gaye tunes at too high of a volume. Straight out of a defensive driving course, Eazy is almost ran into by one of Los Angeles's many Latino drivers, after his near brush with the law. At this point, he has also polished off the Olde English he was drinking and must stop at the store for more. In an awful conclusion to the many challenges that E has already faced since leaving the house, he now spots someone trying to break into the trunk of his car, while re-stocking his liquor supply in the store. Eazy believes that seeing him drunk while exiting his car gave the intruder confidence to commit such an act. E responds by firing his gun and scaring off the thief, rounding out the second verse.

Eric begins the third verse with a clarification for anyone confused about the street vernacular, which gives the song its title, stating "Olde English 800, cause that's my brand." Suggesting that he is open to having the beverage in any available quantity, he then goes on to espouse his disdain for California penal code 502, drunk driving. Finally, Eazy makes it to the party that we assume he has been headed to since the song began, only to be refused a dance, told his breath smells, and eventually vomiting in the parking lot. He does regain some of his dignity by the verse's end, when he drops a partygoer who appears to be disapproving too loudly of Eazy's behavior.

The song is rounded out with a roll call of a few of Eazy's (and perhaps more presumably Ice Cube's friends). Ron De Vu, who did lyrical duty with Eazy-E on a few earlier cuts, Dr. Dre, and Cube's old rapping partners, CIA, are given shout outs. As is Krazy D, the early latino N.W.A. member who appears on the cover of N.W.A. and the Posse and received a writing credit on Panic Zone, a song on that same album. A line from the final bars of the song would come back to later haunt Eazy, after he and Cube were no longer on speaking terms. "Ice

Cube writes the rhymes, that I'll say," admits Eazy. Cube would later go on to sample this admission and use it to torment N.W.A. on records, where he questioned their lyrical abilities and earlier success, attributing it to his own rhyme skills.

Dre's production on 8 Ball weaves together a wide array of different musical styles and contributors, only possible before the sample-clearing craze that presides over music presently. Snippets and interpolations of "It's My Beat" by Sweet Tea, "Be Thankful for What You Got" by William Devaughn, "Yes, We Can Can" by Pointer Sisters "(You Gotta) Fight for Your Right (To Party!)", "The New Style", "Girls", "Paul Revere", and "Hold It, Now Hit It" by Beastie Boys, "Terminator X Speaks With His Hands" by Public Enemy, "Too Much Posse" by Public Enemy, "Hollywood Swinging" by Kool & the Gang, "Let's Get It On" by Marvin Gaye, "Go See the Doctor" by Kool Moe Dee, "Boyz-n-the-Hood" by Eazy-E, "My Melody" by Eric B. & Rakim can all be heard.

"8 Ball" doesn't really give us any new information about N.W.A. on *Straight Outta Compton*. However, we must remember that it wasn't new when the album was released, since fans were already familiar with the cut from N.W.A. and the Posse. What the song does serve as is a brick in the wall of identity and image that the group was constructing on the seminal album. Without these solid bricks, a group's image loosely hangs around one or two singles.

Lyrics for the Adults

Something Like That

N.W.A. always had a penchant for referencing, remixing and referring to their previous material. It was actually a brilliant strategy as it conveyed a high level of importance and notoriety to the songs they had previously released, causing many to constantly be purchasing their back catalogue and looking for the material they referenced in their current material.

"Something Like That," is in a way a "sequel" to another song on *Straight Outta Compton*: "Compton's in Da House." Perhaps Dr. Dre intended for "Compton's in Da House" to be included on the *N.W.A. and the Posse* E.P. or some other N.W.A. related project that had not yet come to fruition. Regardless, both songs appeared on the same album, with "Something Like That" ironically appearing on the album *before* "Compton's in Da House." To be fair, "Compton's in Da House" is listed on the album as a remix, calling into question our previous inquiry, since the original mix of "Compton's in Da

House" does not appear on any released N.W.A. material before *Straight Outta Compton* or since.

The song begins with a verbal exchange between Dr. Dre and MC Ren, asking each other if they are ready to perform. They then make a request of group member DJ Yella to give them a drum beat, which despite having the title of DJ, seems to be Yella's most significant contribution to the group's music on the album. The duo then give a couple of shout outs to Eazy-E, who appears to be in the studio during the recording, and then all of Compton, who do not. Dre then asks what they should call the song, suggesting the title "Tell 'Em What Your Name Is." Ren responded with the phrase that must have won out for the song's title, "Something Like That."

The first verse is delivered by Ren, who interestingly invokes a concern for us as the general public and our rights to information. He states, "You are the public, you should know what's up." Ren also mentions early on that "Compton's in Da House was more than gold, it was a hit, / cause it was based on some crazy shit." While being an interesting statement and rhyme, it is verifiably wrong on all accounts. First, the original mix of the song does not appear on any of the group's previous material, much less any material that sold 500,000 copies, certifying it gold. It was not a hit by any account and if the remix is any indication, the subject material is fairly mundane and definitely not based on any "crazy shit." Dre soon comes in apparently attempting to get his way with the song's title and theme, suggesting Ren "Tell 'em what your name is."

Ren takes Dre's suggestion and delivers, but his next reference is one of the most unlikely on the album. He compares himself to James Arness's character on the TV western, "Gunsmoke." However, he is quick to point out the key difference between the two, being Matt Dillon is a man of the law and he is not. Ren finishes up his verse with much of his usual bravado and then tag teams Dre with a line that surely must have pleased the good Doctor, "Tell 'em what your name is."

Dre then begins his verse, written, as much of his material was, by The D.O.C. Amidst his lyrics, he makes an odd pronouncement of humility, "Never saying I'm the best, I'm just going for mine." This is by far the most interesting part of Dre's verse, because it is so off color compared to the normal braggadocio making up most of hip-hop's lyrical canon at the time, including *Straight Outta Compton*. Soon after, Dre abruptly ends his verse.

Ren steps in with another verbal exchange outside the realm of the lyrical, letting Dre know that he needs to add a few more bars to complete his verse. Dre agrees and the two emcees finish the song together a la the style we hear on the remix of "Compton's in Da House." The song's finale ends much as it begins with a verbal exchange between our two lyricists, mentioning Eazy-E and Yella have remained with us throughout the completion of the song. It seems that Ice Cube and Arabian Prince have now joined us in the studio as well. Finally, Dre does something rarely heard on N.W.A. material and gives a shout out to an act in no way affiliated with N.W.A., a competing group from the same neighborhood, CMW (Compton's Most Wanted).

Besides Yella's drum beat, the musical samples on the cut are courtesy of Fat Larry's Band's "Down on the Avenue," The Steve Miller Band's "Take the Money and Run," and Z.Z. Hill's "I Think I'd Do It." While certainly not the most memorable cut on the album, "Something Like That" is a throwback to old school hip-hop style, when emcees rapped together in a singsong-like style and shared verses instead of demanding their own. Ultimately, the group would not be able to contain the strong personalities of Ice Cube and Eazy-E, who almost always needed their own verses to shine. While the song is missing the verbal cleverness of Cube and the magical voice of Eazy, it does represent something unique N.W.A was bringing to the table at a time when no other group on the west coast could—a unified vision unconcerned about any one person getting all the credit, in favor of a powerful collective.

—JKB

Lyrics for the Adults

Express Yourself

Widely considered N.W.A.'s first radio-friendly single, "Express Yourself" is actually a cover of Charles Wright and the Watts 103rd Street Rhythm Band's song of the same name. The tune remains one of the more interesting anomalies on *Straight Outta Compton*. For starters, it is the only song on the album fully lyrically manned by none of N.W.A.'s chief lyricists, but instead by producer Dr. Dre. It should be noted that Ice Cube and Eazy-E are given writing credits on the song and that a remix version used in the video for the song features brief lyrical tags by Cube and MC Ren. Next, the song thematically challenges just about everything the group professes on the rest of the album. Finally, "Express Yourself" is profanity and violence free.

The record opens with a brief *a cappella* conversation between Dr. Dre and Ice Cube.

[Dr. Dre:] *Yo, man... There's a lot of brothers out there flakin' and perpetratin' but scared to kick reality.*
[Ice Cube:] *Man, you've been doing all this dope producin', you haven't had a chance to show 'em what time it is...*

[Dr. Dre:] *So, what you want me to do?*

Everything appears to be on course for another N.W.A. tale about the reality of the streets and the lives of gangstas, bitches, and hoes. Then, without warning, a classic pop hook is brought in about creative expression. Immediately, we assume Dre is using the hook in some ironic twist to juxtapose hard lyrics with inspirational music, as he explores on Eazy-E's "We Want Eazy." He begins:

I'm expressin' with my full capabilities,
And now I'm livin' in correctional facilities,
Cause some don't agree with how I do this.

The assumption seems to be playing out as expected. This will be a tale of a gangsta locked up for his evil deeds. Dre proceeds:

I get straight, meditate like a Buddhist
I'm droppin' flava, my behavior is hereditary,
But my technique is very necessary.
Blame it on Ice Cube... Because he says it gets funky
When you got a subject and a predicate.

Not even the most astute hip hop philosopher could make sense out of where Dre may be going with this progression. Common lyrical braggadocio moves the track along until we get to the true showstopper on the track. Dre, now infamously announces:

I still express, yo, I don't smoke weed or sess.
Cause its known to give a brother brain damage.
And brain damage on the mic don't manage nuthin'
But makin' a sucker and you equal.
Don't be another sequel.

It should be noted at this point in N.W.A.'s lyrical canon, marijuana was not a major theme, especially in positive terms. Other than the occasional reference, their song "Dopeman" was the only real area where they discussed weed. Ironically, that record presents drugs in quite a negative tone, especially in Cube's final verse. It was not shocking that N.W.A. seemed to be expressing anti-drug sentiment, as even hard core groups such as Run D.M.C. had made similar statements on records. What was shocking was N.W.A.'s seeming attempt to be positive and inspirational. This seemed contradictory to most of the rest of the music N.W.A. had made up to this point.

Over the years, several "water cooler theories" surfaced about "Express Yourself." Perhaps N.W.A.

was making a positive turn and this was the last record made for the album. It was the last single released from *Straight Outta Compton*. Perhaps N.W.A. didn't themselves really believe any of what they said on the record and it was merely an act. Perhaps the record company had forced them to do something radio friendly. After all, Dre does appear to be wavering a bit on the group's new image presentation claiming:

Some musicians curse at home
But scared to use profanity
When up on the microphone.
Yeah, they want reality.
But you won't hear none.
They rather exaggerate, a little fiction.

In a note of true irony, N.W.A. appeared to be reluctant to use profanity when upon the microphone for this song, whatever the underlying reason was. They do seem to want to assure us that they will not be abandoning the "reality" topics but then immediately return to the anti-drug messages and the hypocrisy surrounding them. Making it clear that they might not be down with dope, but they remain strong supporters of the second amendment. Dre says:

Lyrics for the Adults

Some say no to drugs and take a stand,
But after the show they go lookin' for the dopeman.

And then later:

And if you start fessin'
I got a Smith and Wesson for you

While the song continues this thematic see saw, there is one final lyrical gem worth noting. At one point in the song, Dre makes the statement, "N.W.A. is the lynch mob!" A couple of years later, Ice Cube would leave N.W.A. and refer to his new posse' as Da Lench Mob. When this occurred, there was some speculation that Cube's break with N.W.A. was a media stunt and naming his new crew Da Lench Mob was a reference to this lyric in "Express Yourself." However, listeners soon realized that since Cube was likely the author of "Express Yourself," he wrote the lyric and likely just liked the term.

"Express Yourself" would be re-made by no less than three other bands in the coming years. The remakes would be covers of N.W.A.'s version of the song and not the original by Charles Wright and the Watts 103rd Street Rhythm Band. The cut remains the only N.W.A. song to receive regular rotation on the radio and video markets. However, most analysts would argue that the radio-friendly single did absolutely nothing to boost album sales, as the N.W.A. featured on "Express Yourself" was really not the N.W.A. people wanted to hear. Dre and the group must have received the message, as they never released another record in a similar vein, and spent significant moments in their careers (especially Dre) having to defend the song—and take heat for its positive vibe.

—JKB

Lyrics for the Adults

Compton's in the House

A solo bass beat. A kick drum, two men, and a microphone. A highly scripted rehearsal posing as improvisation. St-st-st-stutter steppin to the first lyric. To the people over here to the people over there—people apparently at an N.W.A. concert "paying top dollar." The track tries to establish the feel of being in the recording studio, just hanging out (a device also used at the beginning of "Parental Discretion iz Advised").

Many of the rhymes on this track are oft-repeated elsewhere on the album (rage/twelve-gauge, sucka/muthafucka, luck/fuck), adding up to a pedestrian, workmanlike collection on top of that stripped-down beat, but that's sort of the point. This is gangsta rap in its purest form. Vitriol *qua* vitriol. Personalities it is assumed the listener is already familiar with. The overwhelming consistent theme being WE WILL FUCK YOU UP. Not to say that there aren't some innovative attempts at rhyme—for example, rhyming coroner/foreigner and twilight/my fight. Sadly, Ren seems to shine in places where the spotlight hides. His verses in the title track and "Fuck tha Police" are not as solid.

Compton pride dominates the message of the track and of the album. And yet this pride-of-place is really nothing new in rap, in music, in language. One of the first (if not *the* first) rap hit single was the Sugar Hill Gang's "Rapper's Delight"—Sugar Hill being a small neighborhood in Harlem (New York, NY). Representing one's city or neighborhood is paramount to the success of any group. Location trumps all. East Coast vs. West Coast. The ATL—STL connection. Oakland. Staten Island/Shaolin. The Fifth Ward. Hollis, Queens. The list goes on. N.W.A. took this focus on geography and lifted it (and Compton) into the stratosphere. Almost everyone who saw Eazy-E and Ice Cube and even the D.O.C. wearing LA Raiders and LA Kings hats immediately wanted to copy them.

The cassette and CD cover photography and music videos of N.W.A. were crucial in the portrayal of the "real" Compton. I would submit that the desire to see life on the streets in Compton (or at least South Central L.A.) is what fueled the success of John Singleton's 1991 hit film "Boyz N the Hood." The film earned Singleton Oscar nominations for Best Director and Best Original Screenplay.

Lyrics for the Adults

In the English language, insistence on representing ones place of origin dates at least back to Beowulf, who wore the "gang colors" of the Geats—eventually becoming king of all Geats.

The maps created a thousand years ago that demarcated the boundaries between the Geats, the Wulfings, the Swedes, the Jutes, the Danes, etc. are no different than the mental maps rap fans form of where their favorite rappers hail from (this mapping of the United States has given prominence not only to names of specific neighborhoods, but also the area code map). The importance of the place of origin takes on a greater significance when there are journeys to and from the battlefield, journeys that take the soldier out of his homeland and into foreign lands—a defense of Herot in Beowulf's case, and unwitting success with and travels into white suburbia in N.W.A.'s case.

N.W.A.'s journey from Compton ghetto to the white suburbs is as complex as Beowulf's journey into Herot hall because the success of the group depends on establishing themselves as credible gangsters from an evil place. No one would fear a gangster from the suburbs of Wichita or downtown Burbank—the persona relies on the place of origin being sufficiently intimidating to the Other. The epic hero, be it Beowulf or Eazy-E, lives and dies by his locally established reputation—and his capacity for violence.

Many residents of Compton and South Central Los Angeles protested the portrayal of their community as unadulterated evil, a gangster's paradise. To them, the portrayal was not only insulting and regressive, it was flat out incorrect. Now, twenty years later, the damage has been done. The name *Compton* seems irrevocably linked to drive-by shootings, drug-dealing, and ruthless gangs. Actual corruption by the Compton Police Department (which forced the department to disband in 2000) cannot help. At this point in history, the reputation of Compton and South Central seems lost for good. Has the name *Watts* changed connotations in 40 years? Not to white suburbia. N.W.A.'s argument is to flip this negativity around and capitalize on the reputation and, it seems, eventually move out of the 'hood.

Throughout this track, Ren and Dre take turns extolling the murderous virtues of their hometown. But the turns are more like separate tracks. The tone and direction first slightly changes with "Speakin' of Compton, it's makin' me sick [why?]" as if Dre walked into a rap about Compton and thought, oh yeah! speaking of Compton... And then they decide to rhetorically sing out *a la* Biz Markie or Fila Fresh Crew: "WHAT DO YOU CALL A CREW THAT CAN RAP LIKE THAT?" What indeed.

The next turn is a weird pastiche of a "verse" that starts with a sample from Dana Dane's *Cinderfella* ("Hell no, he replied"), samples of Dre talking about Dre, samples Ren talking about Ren, and then transitions into some hardcore pontificating by a "nigga in black," MC Ren. Then, Dre interrupts Ren with a "Who really cares..." and the track ends not with a bang but with a whimper of "Compton, Compton, Compton, Compton."

It should be noted that the title of the track is somewhat lightweight—"in the house" being passé even at the time the record was released. The LL Cool J/Maia Campbell TV series "In the House" on the WB (1995) was the death knell in any remaining cool-factor left in the phrase, reeking of a white executive's attempt to be cool and label a black show. The origin of the phrase is unclear, but the popularization of it by Arsenio Hall in introducing his guests greatly contributed to its usage during this time ("We got Johnny Gill in the house tonight!! Yesssss!").

—MBB

Lyrics for the Adults

I Ain't Tha 1

Although N.W.A. was thought to be one of the most misogynistic groups of their time, only one song on their most noted album was devoted to the subject of the opposite sex. It should be noted that as many songs were about dancing on *Straight Outta Compton* as were about dealing with females, though the latter subject certainly was mentioned throughout the album than the former. It should also be noted that "I Ain't tha 1" was Ice Cube's solo contribution to the album as each member represented only themselves on at least one track on the album (save for DJ Yella). Finally, it is interesting to note that the song was narrowly chosen to appear on the album over Cube's other solo recorded cut "A Bitch Iz A Bitch," which later appeared as a 12 inch single B-side. That track turned out to be much more of a fan favorite than Cube's discussion of male female relationships that did appear on *Straight Outta Compton*, though both songs deal with similar subject matter.

Many N.W.A songs begin with some spoken phrase, discussion, or bit. "I Ain't tha 1" is no exception. The song opens with a young woman asking Ice Cube for money to get her hair and nails done. Cube responds in song seemingly right out of a Broadway musical. "I ain't the one, the one to get played like a pooh-butt." He goes on to describe the games he feels women play teasing him with their sexuality to get his money. He is upfront that sex is clearly all he desires from these women, so the situation creates tension. He goes on the claim that he is above these games and while he might end up getting sex from a woman, she will clearly not get what she desires, if that desire is financial.

Much of what makes *Straight Outta Compton* critically acclaimed is its timelessness. Only occasionally does N.W.A. drop pop references that date their material throughout the album. Cube does recall the fashion of the time stating that girls in biker's shorts (look so fly to me." While girls in biker's shorts might still get wanting stares from current hip hop culture, the fashion trend is clearly dissipated. Throughout the track Cube offers timeless sentiments that have been discussed throughout the ages by men taking issues with the fairer gender. "When it comes to sex, she's got a bad cough, or a headache," Cube states. Volumes of literature, television shows and films have made light of these stereotypical excuses some women have given for not being intimate.

Lyrics for the Adults

The chorus of the song is again a departure for Dr. Dre, as well as the rest of N.W.A.. Instead of any sort of chant or sampled phrase, we again hear the young woman who opens the song plainly speak about her view of the situation. She makes no attempt to musically incorporate her thoughts into the song. Instead we are led to believe that we are overhearing her speaking candidly with one of her girlfriends. Her candid remarks directly reinforce the simple point Cube continues to drive home throughout the song.

The rapper seems to let his more vulnerable side show on the second verse, demonstrating his naiveté before he "figured out the game." He wonders," How the hell an ugly dude get a fine girls number?" He quickly surmises from the situation that the man in question is being "juiced for his ducats." As a point of order, it should be pointed out that "ducats" were commonly used in hip hop slang at the time and referred to a type of gold coin that was used as currency in several European countries. He goes on to rhymes that he drives a "bucket," another interesting slang term used at the time referring to an older car with bucket seats. With all the hurt feelings of a good man scorned, Cube rationalizes the reason he refuses to bring flowers to a girl on a date is that she would "take it for granted, no doubt." He completes the second verse reinforcing his near superhero-like ability to resist the kryptonite that is "big ole butts."

Cube does not offer much in the way of new material in the third and final verse of the song. He basically finds new ways to restate the thesis he has already laid out. He does offer advice for women wanting to avoid the situation suggesting, "You shouldn't be so damn material." In a statement that seems quite out of character with the rest of the song, Cube warns, "If I have to go get a gun, you girls will learn." While, certainly not a romantic cut, this is really the only threat of violence against women in the song. It is curious that for the most part, Cube plays the part of the victim in the song. Time and again he suggests that women are the ones who began this cycle and that his responses are merely reactionary to the plotting by his would be suitors.

Musically, "I Ain't tha 1" relies on one sample looped and sectioned apart. "The Message (Inspiration)" by Brass Construction provides the entire musical background over a simple beat constructed by Dre. This was a common formula for the good Doctor at the time, as well as for many of hip hop's elite producers. Other cuts on Straight Outta Compton such as "Parental Discretion Iz Advised," "Express

Yourself," and "Dopeman" were similarly constructed around one little known sample.

The song concludes as it opens with the young woman pulling the love card on Cube. He retorts and thus gets the last word telling the woman to "beat it." Interestingly, before the departure, he does mention that there is no ring on his finger. This would lead one to imply that courtesy of Cube's philosophy, a married man would be in a position to give the woman in question money for her requests and not be surprised when sex is not available from her. Again, this notion seems pulled from the hat of any of today's top stand up comedians. Though not the most memorable song on the album, "I Ain't tha 1" does provide a great deal of insight into the mindset N.W.A. held regarding relationships. These ideals would be explored many times over in other song by the band and by hip hop music at large. — JKB

Lyrics for the Adults

Something 2 Dance 2

"Something 2 Dance 2" is likely the most puzzling cut on *Straight Outta Compton*. Though Ice Cube opened this album with the line "Here's a murder rap to keep y'all dancing." This was the only cut that really delivered on that promise. It is the thirteenth cut on the album so it is unlikely that N.W.A. need the track to meet some sort of contractual obligation with Priority. It is also unlikely that they did not have other material to choose from to complete the album. As has been discussed, Ice Cube had "A Bitch iz a Bitch," later to become a sleeper hit for the group, ready to be released. Most likely, the song represents the group's noble attempts at fairness and the power of friendship.

Despite the fact that the track was unlike anything else on the rest of the album, and despite the fact that the musical style was diametrically opposed to everything else they were putting forth, it is most likely that the group had allotted one solo track on the album to each member. DJ Yella had not produced any solo material at that point so his contribution stood musically on several other tracks.

However, Arabian Prince had been involved as a member of N.W.A. since its inception. He brought more danceable music and represented what Dr. Dre and Yella had been involved with from their roots with The World Class Wrecking Crew. Despite making the album cover photo, he had not contributed anything else to *Straight Outta Compton.* "Something 2 Dance 2" would be his sole contribution to the album.

It should be noted, however, that other members of the group took one for the team and participated vocally on the song, in what must have been an attempt to give the song some cohesion with the rest of the album. Despite these attempts, the record was never released as a single and received virtually no club play, despite its danceable beat. While mostly programmed on Arabian Prince's Roland TR-808 drum machine, elements of "Dance to the Music" by Sly and the Family Stone as well as "You're the One For me" by D-Train can be clearly heard as well.

While it would be easy to write off this track as a throw away that N.W.A. should have left off the album for thematic reasons alone, the song represents something that was culturally important to hip hop and perhaps an element that truly makes the album a classic to purists. First, the subject matter of the song appears to be moot. However, upon further examination, one can easily recognize the importance of dance clubs to West coast hip hop.

Other street-reality based acts such as Ice T started out performing in similar scenes and making music for the clubs. And while the music was made for dancing, it was the lyrics that were different. It was the subject matter that set the music apart from other music being played at west coast dance clubs. Gangsters of the era did not shy away from appearances at dance clubs as was often celebrated lyrically. It was usually made clear that these settings were connecting with the opposite sex and not dancing, as dancing had not been en vogue for gangsters since breakdancing ruled the clubs.

Even in the sparse lyrics that make up the song we hear, "What? You want to leave? With all these females on my sleeve?" It was clear that dance music had a direct connection to getting girls. This being the case, "Something 2 Dance 2," does have a direct thematic connection to the rest of the album, perhaps less pronounced than in "I Ain't tha One." But a connection none the less.

The musical style of the song also represents the transition from the more electronic sound that exemplified west coast hip hop to the more raw sound that Dr. Dre had begun to produce. And although

N.W.A. may not have been the first to bring an electronic danceable sound to hip hop nor a raw big beat, as was being brought by rappers such as King T and Mixmaster Spade at the time; they may well have been the first to bring both on one album. And the fact that only one electronic dance song is represented along side the other 12 raw based beats, may well represent the death of electronic dance music as the official soundtrack of gangsters and the birth of raw more organic beats to represent that culture. We literally see this transition happen on *Straight Outta Compton*.

In *Straight Outta Compton*'s era, cassette tapes ruled the musical scene and "Something 2 Dance 2" was the final song on the album. Many, if not most, listeners fast forwarded through the song to get to one of the best Side 1 Song 1's in all of hip hop, "Straight Outta Compton." Others simply turned the cassette over when the song came on to catch "Fuck tha Police."

However, in the eyes of this author, this song was something special. It represented one of the last big chances N.W.A. took as a group. It demonstrated a fun and playful side of this group with no violence. While the cut would have likely never gotten made if not for the other cuts that made the album famous, it represents a side of the group that we would never see again. Many articles have been written about the skating rinks that N.W.A. played in early on in the career. These were places that gave N.W.A. their start. They were places where a song like "Something 2 Dance 2" would have been just as popular as "Fuck the Police." Most that has been written about the group is also quick to point out the fact that the hardcore content and lifestyle N.W.A. rapped about came second hand from people they knew and things they saw as opposed to things they experienced. It might be fair to say that the final cut on *Straight Outta Compton* gave us a quick but rare glimpse into who the rappers really were and not just who they wanted us to believe they were.

—JKB

Part II
The Interviews

Interview with Eric Poppelton

Eric Poppelton served as photographer for the cover of Straight Outta Compton *and* Eazy-Duz-It. *He lives in Los Angeles, California.*

John Bucher: So this album was one of your first photo shoots?

Eric Poppelton: Well, we were straight out of Cal Arts, myself and Kevin Hosmann. He's an art director friend of mine from Cal Arts. We graduated in 1986 and I was going to ask you, when was that album cover published? Was it '88 or '86?

JB: '88

EP: '88, so the year after we had graduated. He [Hosmann] was the one who was asked to be the creative director. I think he was working at Capital Records at the time. So we were doing this as a freelance project. He got the ball rolling, asked me to be the photographer. This was literally one of our quote bigger jobs and now at the time I was still assisting Penny Wollen at that phase. So it was great, how we got to direct and do our own thing. But to be honest with you, we didn't know anything about locations, getting proper permits, all that kind of stuff. We just kind of went mid-week and just basically ripped all these locations and just did these things, you know it was insane. It was the middle of the night, it was always middle of the night. We had no clue who these guys all were. They were just like us, just fresh out of school and they were just starting out. Had I known where it was gonna go, and obviously no one can predict that, like the stock market, things could have been different. This was also my only involvement with music photography at all, doing these albums covers.

JB: So when he told you the name of the group, did you try and get any ideas about where to shoot?

EP: Most of that was left up to Kevin, and I helped pick the locations and obviously the compositions and where to put people and all that kind of stuff. It was really a collaborative process between myself and Kevin. He had the overall ideas and I made sure it looked good. Like I said, we were just making up stuff. We were using car headlights and these old strobes, like a strobe you could put a slide in so you could project images on the ceilings and bottoms of bridges. It was just nuts. We were putting generators in places we shouldn't have. I couldn't imagine doing it nowadays. I would have had like four or five cops doing something like that now. It was a bad part of downtown L.A. that's for sure.

JB: Did you do the photography also for Eazy-E's *Eazy-Duz-It?*

EP: I believe so. There were four or five album covers I recall us doing. And everyone calls me and they're like, do you have any of the old artwork? It's not like today when you have digital copies, all the transparencies went right to the client. You know all the other stuff that hits the cutting room floor, its just gone. And its really kind of a drag, because I've been called I don't know how many times in the past 3 or 4 years, do you have any of those old slides? They're incredible. I shot them all in a hospital because you know I'm a freak about being tack sharp, I mean technically perfect and all that other stuff. They're great and they're somewhere, maybe someone's scanned them by now, but I don't know.

JB: Now tell me a little bit about the beginning of this shoot. Is there anything in particular about this one? Did the guys show up on time? What was the atmosphere on the set like?

EP: They were really reliable as I recall. They were really reliable. Also, I never like heard their music until like two years later. Yeah, I had no clue, they just never played it when I was around. I knew what the album was called, I knew what the band was called. I was dating an African-American female at the time, I'm this white guy from the Midwest, and first of all I get plugged down at Cal Arts, which is a mixed bag of people from all over the world. I don't really consider myself racist or whatever, so you know we're just doing our job you know. After we did that album cover, I was interviewed by VH1 a few years ago, myself and Kevin, and they told me the controversy that album stirred up and I had no clue. Until that day I had no clue, and this is years later they were telling me this. I didn't feel really great about that. And I still don't know the full story about how controversial it was, but while we were there it was fine.

JB: So, they were easy to work with?

EP: Yeah, they were all easy going, and like I said we were all starting out at the same time. It was pretty amazing collaborative, I mean even with them you know. They were game to anything that we asked them to do and they would stay the whole time and it didn't seem to be like this whole big crowd. We were focused on what we were doing—that was our thing.

JB: Were any of the band members involved in choosing what ended up on the album cover? Or was it the record company?

EP: I don't have any idea honestly, it was probably the record company.

JB: I don't know if you remember, but in this particular shot, you were laying on the ground with these guys over you, can you tell us a little bit about how this was set up?

EP: I remember we were walking down an alley, I'm sure Kevin and I were just talking like "hey, what about this?" I just laid down on the ground, and probably shot it with a 24mm, and I wasn't afraid. I'm sure I asked them if the gun had bullets in it or not, typical, obviously, and I'm sure it was real. I mean I didn't inspect it, because we at that point, we had done a couple of album covers for them before that, and it was really a great relationship. So, I wish it would have continued, but obviously at some point they got bigger and they chose a different art director and photographer to go with the rest of their career.

JB: In that shot [the cover of *Straight Outta Compton*], did they bring the gun with them?

EP: I'm sure they did. Because I know we didn't bring anything like that. No, I definitely didn't bring that.

JB: They had their own guns.

EP: And maybe well I'm not gonna say anything, I don't know.

JB: Well, you know, he's [Eazy-E] passed away now.

EP: That's true.

JB: Was all this in downtown Los Angeles?

EP: Everything was shot in downtown LA. Even the barbershop scene, which I'm sure you're aware of. I couldn't remember if we drove around or not, but that wasn't actually a barbershop, it was a shoeshine shop. And that was an actual shoeshine shop somewhere in downtown Los Angeles. And that one I think we purely made up on the fly. You'd have to ask [Hosmann]. I remember a lot of times just kinda walking around. We were just making it up.

JB: What was the first time that you realized, maybe even after the fact, that this was a big deal.

EP: Well, two things I guess. One, I went to Santa Fe photo workshops, to be an assistant instructor in 1990. And I was driving, at the time I was still photographing people, and so I pulled into this little town outside Taos, New Mexico, and a bunch of kids, like 12-15 year old kids at this gas station... Well, see, I was in the habit of just driving around by myself and asking people if I could take their portrait. I had all black and white, two-and-a-quarter stuff, and these kids were playing one of their albums, and I was like, "What is this?" And they told me it was N.W.A. and I said no way. And we'd already been working there like 15, 20 minutes and I said I did their album covers and they freaked out. They're like no you didn't, so I pulled a business card out, and I flipped over the album cover and said, look, this is me. Then they were all over me, asking me all kinds of questions. I can't remember exactly how the conversation went, but that was the first time I heard the music.

JB: That's interesting, because I know that a lot of groups now, when they're doing their album covers, they play their music. It wasn't the case in the beginning.

EP: None of it. It was a serious photo shoot. Back then I didn't even know how we would play the music. We didn't even have power on those shoots. There was not a flash on that one in particular. No, we brought power to some of it, but I don't recall them ever playing the music. I don't know why Kevin and I didn't ever discuss that. I'm sure Kevin knew it, he had to do more of the typeface decisions, and that kind of thing. Yeah I never heard it.

JB: Were the guys serious the whole time, were they joking around at all?

EP: You know, it wasn't that serious, because sometimes we had to make them serious. Like this one cover that we did was under a bridge. And we had a bunch of cars lighting them and then all these strobes and all these effects that were going off, because that was the attitude that they wanted to give off. But other than that, I don't remember going to dinner or having drinks with them afterwards.

JB: You said that Kevin was very instrumental in composing a lot of the shots. Were these scenes well thought out? I'm fascinated by how you said so much of it was just on the fly. Because so much of it has just become cultural, iconic, even this photograph is on millions of albums.

EP: Right.

JB: Its on a million different albums covers. Its everywhere and its very iconic. And the Eazy-E photograph that you're talking about with the car light behind it under the bridge—its very iconic stuff. Totally on the fly, though?

EP: Totally on the fly. I don't remember ever going and scouting before. But I, it was a longtime ago now.

JB: How long did a shoot like this last?

EP: Just about two to four hours. I mean I'm sure if I had all the film I could tell you exactly, because we went to 10 or 8 different spots. And they weren't more than half a day, ever. You know maybe the all-night shoot was a little bit more, because it was a little more involved. But none of them were more than a half day I'm sure.

JB: The shoot under the bridge, with the car lights and all that, you know Eazy-E's album cover. I never even realized that was under a bridge, and I looked at that album cover like a million times. I always thought they were in some kind of cave or a dark lair of some kind. One thing I noticed about that album cover though is how well-lit he is, and the other guys are kind of in the background. But one of the things that had been discussed about the group, is because there have been so many people from the group that have gone on to make big names for themselves, was there ever any discussion or tension on set about who was more prominently featured? Did they have discussions among themselves, do you recall?

EP: They might well have done that. They might have talked with Kevin about that. And I'm sure Kevin must have picked the orientation. But I don't know on that one, though. I think they just kind of grouped together. Man, that's so long ago, I can't be sure. I'm sure Kevin discussed it with them. He must have.

JB: In the shot its kind of interesting that, in a way, you can't really even see their faces, but again its become so iconic, them standing over you. Did it strike you that this is not ideally photographic?

EP: Yeah, and it's a tough situation, because technically it's backlit, if you use some kind of a flash it would throw it off. I'm sure we didn't have that in mind. So obviously, if I would have had more of an opportunity to light it I would have. I'm sure that was just available light. There may have been a fill card laying down there that probably Kevin was holding. Who knows? But back then I was like the commercial photographer. I was just out of art school and I knew X amount. If I knew what it was now, it definitely wouldn't have looked that way. But, talking to the point of how it does look? I'm sure its become a topic of discussion of why it looks that way.

JB: It has. It certainly has. It's kind of one of those situations where people writing about it, there was a lot more thought put into it than it sounds like there actually was.

EP: I wish there were. Yeah, I think people were thinking too hard about that. I mean, I think that's the thing about a photograph, you have time to study it. And there's no words, so they're thinking back to what we might have been thinking about them, where I wasn't trying to make any statement about these guys, at all. We were just like, "hey, this might work." And back then, in the transparency material, the latitude of film was this much compared to what we do now. So, it wasn't intentionally dark.

JB: That's interesting, because a lot people that say this is very much a crafted image, and it looks like it's not.

EP: Nope. It's not.

JB: One reason I'm sure a lot of people contact you is to find out if there are any more images, because these images have become so iconic. Do you recall when you were shooting this session, does it even goes through your head this is a real keeper?

EP: No, because when you shoot people, you're rattling off lots of frames. I mean, all the good stuff, especially when you're shooting 35mm, there's that instant when the shutter releases and you don't see. You know, if you don't see anything, then you probably got something really great. I used to shoot a lot of sports, you go to basketball, you name it, you got to a football game, if you saw the game through your lens, you missed it. You completely missed it. At the end, you should recall nothing. And that's the way a 35mm works. You might be able to do a Polaroid in advance, to set your composition and your lighting and what not, which we didn't have the ability to do with 35 and that's like the next step up, like two-and-a-quarter stuff. So again, if you saw it, you missed it. So, it wasn't until afterwards, well now with digital its obvious you can see it right away, but its never until you get your film back that you started to reveal what was really in the shoot.

JB: Any other little stories that you might remember? Anything that happened during any of the shoots that that strikes you?

EP: It was just fun. It was just great to have work. And get paid for something you really had a free hand in. And it was great working with Kevin. It was just Kevin and Eric then. We had no idea what the exposure was going to do, and they didn't either.

It would have been nice to have gone along the way, a little bit more, but it didn't happen.

JB: They only put out one other album after this actually.

EP: Together.

JB: Together. Before they all went their separate ways. That album cover [*Niggaz4Life*], interestingly enough, is not considered very iconic in hip hop culture. It's got them laying dead on the ground, with their ghosts coming up out of the ground.

EP: Oh I didn't do that one.

JB: Its funny because it [*Niggaz4Life*] is remembered as being not who the group was. So when people think of who the group was, the only images that they ever point to were the images that you shot for their album covers—and the shoeshine scene and things like that. Some of those shots that didn't make the album covers, but were on the covers of 12-inch singles and things like that that. That's the iconic era.

EP: Thanks. It's too bad how they ended up.

Lyrics for the Adults

Interview with Kevin Hosmann

Kevin Hosmann is a designer. He served as art director and graphic designer for the cover of Straight Outta Compton, Eazy-Duz-It, *Ice Cube's* Death Certificate, *and many other iconic hip hop albums.*

John Bucher: So what was the general concept of the cover of *Straight Outta Compton*?

Kevin Hosmann: Well, with that shot right there [the cover image], the idea was basically, they knocked you down, you're in an alley, and you're not coming back up. Right, so the power on top of that. And they thought, that's kind of cool, its interesting and all of that, but what's really interesting when you kind of think about it was Dre is a huge success, one of the biggest producers of all time for black music and Ice Cube is probably one of the most successful black entrepreneurs that had actually become kind of a producer of his own of the movies. He goes out, he makes movies, he makes money on it. He's a crossover star. It's really unfortunate, he he the one who's actually upside down and you're not recognizing his face as much, where the other three on this side, DJ Aladdin was thrown out of the shot. In fact if you look on the back of the cover, you'll actually notice that we retouched him out because he was actually doing a little deal on the side, and Brian Turner was completely pissed off at him. So in some of the shots at the beginning, you'll actually see him in a few other shots, where they're walking with a baseball bat and that through that alley, and magically Arabian Prince was touched out. It was kind of difficult, because again before Photoshop, they actually had to, with an airbrush, completely eliminate this guy. And then Yella is also in there and also Ren, but those guys were really not the powerhouse that the other three were and it was really obvious every time you met them. Ice Cube was really young. He was only 18 and he basically was excited to be there. And Dre really had kind of the power because he was the producer and the sound. And Eric Wright, Eazy-E, he was just basically the skinny guy, little short thing, well a little stocky and wore big jackets, but he really was the power behind that. But he was also kind of this-. He's the kid that probably got hit around on the playground a lot. And that's where he got this kind of, "I got you." You know basically learning how to play it, and Jerry Heller was kind of the money be-

Lyrics for the Adults

hind that and putting it all together. He saw some success there.

JB: Tell me a little bit about the practical atmosphere on the set. Did the guys show up on time? Were they kidding around? Were they easy to work with? Were they always chatting with each other so you had to really corral them? Tell me a little bit about the practical stuff.

KH: What's interesting about the guys in N.W.A. when we actually started doing this is that they just were just like a lot of the other projects that I had. I was very blessed in my record-cover design career in that they all didn't know what they had, and they all didn't know what they would become. And they didn't realize that anyone would care twenty years later. So these guys just showed up. They're completely green kids. When I met Ice Cube for *AmeriKKKa's Most Wanted*, that sea of men, like he orchestrated the gang monster crew of the world. Basically he was organizing all the gangs of Los Angeles. That's what that whole shot was about. That was all shot and re-touched and edited, it was shot in front of his mom's house in Compton. And there's a great interview of Ice Cube as he was just starting to get famous. I think it was Dateline or

NBC, ABC, one of those, where they're walking down the street and the interviewer's going, "Come on Ice Cube, you're talking that you're this gangsta and all of that. Look, this is a *Leave It to Beaver* neighborhood. What are you talking about?" When we went up to Ice Cube's house to set up this shot in front of his house, so all of those guys were there so we could basically cut them out and drop them into *AmeriKKKa's Most Wanted*, I was able to meet his mom and his dad standing there so proudly in the kitchen. And they were just beaming. And his dad— I believe that's actually where *Barbershop* came from, he was actually a barber. He's just a barber from Compton, and here his son is of that success level, he's actually making money at what he wants to do and he's only 18. Think of where he is now and the grand difference of that and becoming a superstar. A true superstar, not just a local hero. But at the very beginning, these guys really didn't know what they had and who they were, or even how to act. They were not that comfortable in front of the camera. They didn't really know what to do. They were kind of posing. If you saw the first N.W.A. cover [*N.W.A. and the Posse*], they're all kind of sitting on that loading dock and they're all doing all their gangs signs and stuff like that. That's kind of what they were emulating, but they didn't really do it in these shots because these were posed. And even the Eric Wright shot that we did for Eazy-E, we did that the very next weekend with the same photographer. And it was just shot, "Bada boom, Bada bing, we got to get outta here," because they weren't going to spend that much money. But by the second album, they were also being photographed by *Rap Pages*. They were getting some press, and also what's the other one, *Rap Pages* and—

JB: *The Source*.

KH: Yeah, *The Source*. Those were the bigger ones, I think *The Source* was even bigger than *Rap Pages*, but I think *Rap Pages* was first. But then what was really funny was, so we graduated from the alley, because they had no money—because if you actually rented a space to actually shoot somewhere it would be 1500 or 2000 dollars. And then all the lighting packages and all of that stuff, so we just called it "run and gun." We went to the alley and we never had permits, as the story goes. We just ran in there and did as many shots as we could with available light and then we went to the next space. And it was because it was so deserted and so fugly that nobody was going to hassle you. So we could easily go get a shot and get back in the car and go somewhere else.

When we actually did get a photoshoot going, a real shoot, where we had lights and we had a studio, by then they had been photographed for quite a while, because they were really getting some press out of it, "Fuck the Police" and all of that from *Nightline*. Or *Dateline*?

JB: I think it was *Nightline*.

KH: *Nightline*, Yeah. Gui Manganiello was the one that actually got that letter. But we're in this photoshoot that was kind of, "Now we've hit the big time." And they were doing all these kind of weird poses. And I saw it again in one of these shots. Just really incredibly obviously weird, stiff poses, and then I realized later that when I was trying to have them, "Hey relax, calm down, you don't have to be so rigid and so tough." They looked uncomfortable. And then I realized that was that kind of a gang posing thing that was evolving and also incorporated from picnic barbecue shots, where these guys would just pose and do all their gang signs and stuff like that. To my knowledge, none of those guys were ever a part of any of that stuff. They were completely clean kids and they were just way into music. And there was another friend of mine, he grew up with those guys. And there was a certain point where he went the opposite way because he was a good, Christian fellow and it was all about bitches and hoes. And Eric [Eazy-E] knew that bitches and hoes kind of dialogue was going to get them the kind of fever and the street credibility. So they were kind of talking this talk of this thing that they, through proximity, they kind of grew up with. It's almost like the wild west, dime store novels from way back when, where turn-of-the-century, it was hyped up just a bit and not all of that stuff really happened, but obviously gangs and bullets do exist. It just wasn't as much in their life as much as they pretended or at least stated in their music. It was all as if they were on the front line, not necessarily with a gun in their hand, but a pen and paper in their hand.

JB: Tell me about this Christian friend that went the other way.

KH: Christian only in the sense. Not to be derogatory in any way, he had values. Steve Wills, it's a weird story, it would take too long to actually understand it.

JB: No, no. Go ahead.

KH: OK, very strange. I used to have all these guys come over to my house because I worked out of my house. [Points to picture of a girl] Ariel here is not mine biologically, I met her and her mom when she was three months old. I asked her to marry me, the mom, Madden, within three weeks, and in four years we had four kids, and we've been married 22 years now. But she always knew that Steve was her biological dad and we always talked about that and it was no secret in any way. One day Steve Wills came over, and Steve Wills is just as tall and as dark as this gentleman right here. And I said, "Hey Steve what's up?" And she looked at Steve and said, "Are you my dad?" And ran and hugged him because she thought that that was Steve. And to my kids, because all of these guys were coming over and you know my mom and dad meeting all of these guys, they didn't see too much difference in, "These were just dad's friends. And we lived in a 1912 Craftsman. And the doors, the French doors on the side were really kind of narrow. And there was this guy, Greedy Greg, a producer, manager or Domino. He actually did platinum or gold at least. He had a big song. And he came over, and Greedy Greg I always thought it was kind of an odd name for a manager, but Greedy Greg was actually a very large gentleman. I said, "So dude, what's with the Greedy and your name for you being a manager, that's not really true, why would you do that?" And he goes. "No, when I was a kid, I ate a lot, and I was a greedy eater. It wasn't the fact that I steal from these guys." But anyway, Greedy Greg would have to go sideways through the door because it was a narrow doorway. And my daughter, who was maybe five at the time, was living in this kind of strange "Dad does rap covers" world. We lived in downtown LA and these guys just walk in and they're always in an entourage of gang-banging looking thugs. It's the look, right? Moreso than anything, they're just doing business. All of these guys, these totally huge gangster-looking thugs come into our house and Madden, my wife, hadn't met them before, didn't know who they were. They were just new clients. And looking down at this little girl it's like, "Why did you let these guys in?" It's like, "Oh no, they're daddy's friends."

To them it was just, "Oh, there's Compton in my room." Anyway, that was kind of funny in that respect. But what was really interesting about working with these guys in the very beginning is that they were truly mining something that was out there. They really knew that there was something out there. And they were really just kind of scribes to it. And they knew how to put a great beat down.

One of the wonderful things about watching the careers of these guys, since seeing Ice Cube in his bedroom at 19 or 18 is that they have really kind of evolved or carried the movement. They weren't just followers after they did this first one. They continued that movement, for Dre it's *The Chronic*, which was a big one for Interscope Records. And then he went into doing Snoop Dogg, which was a huge discovery, and it all just blew up. And then he did Eminem. So that's about fifteen years of real production that is actually an evolution of sound, besides doing Missy Elliot, who was his girlfriend at the time of *Straight Outta Compton* and all that.

JB: At the time, did you have any sense of their music? When you went in to design an album cover, did you listen to some of their music?

KH: I was at Capital Records at the time. I had done MC Hammer, "Let's Get It Started" and I had just done *Paul's Boutique*, the Beastie Boys. There were two divisions, three divisions at Capital Records. There was music, there was country music, and that was Nashville and that was Garth Brooks at the time was making huge money for all of those guys at Capital. And then there was a thing called Black Music, or the black music division. Which I thought was kind of funny, it was basically R&B. Either they called it R&B or they called it black music. Then they all of a sudden had rap. And that was this weird thing that they didn't know how and where to put it.

Capital Records was a total old school label. It was in the tower there at Hollywood and Vine. And they didn't see how any of that could fit into their formula. And so what was happening was that these bands like N.W.A. and any of them that were a bit too progressive, they couldn't put it in a box and they couldn't sell it or promote it either so those guys basically left it alone. But what Priority Records realized is that they could actually promote this stuff and that they could actually get traction by using street vendors, people who at the time, could still cruise Hollywood Boulevard. Now you can't do that. The windows would be rolled down, the music would be belting out, pumping and vibrating. They would throw cassettes through the window and try to get these guys to actually play it in their cars as they were driving down the street. And that's pretty much street promotion, and how it actually started.

They would get these guys, and give street promoters a box of cassettes and hope that they wouldn't just go to the store. Well, actually, they weren't really doing that at the time, but you can sell CDs. It was right at the point that you couldn't sell cassettes. They were all cassettes, they weren't CDs. And they were throwing these things in the cars hoping that they would play them and also that these other guys wouldn't try to sell them. At the time, nobody really wanted any of that crap.

JB: So were you listening along with them then? To this hardcore gangsta rap?

KH: Oh yes, like I said with Capital, it was really kind of tried and true. They had established music on those labels and it was really kind of the end of that kind of corporate rock and they were really floundering. And they really didn't know what was the next thing, because punk and rap was so out there that they didn't really know what to do with it so they didn't touch it.

When you first are put on a project, the first thing is you negotiate a price and you make sure that you're going to get paid. Or at least hope to get paid. The second is you meet with the band and they hand you a tape. It was always a tape. CDs weren't around at the time. So they'd hand you a tape and you'd take a listen to it. When I heard the stuff for N.W.A., I thought, "Oh wow, this is really going to get a lot of radio play," being sarcastic. But what was neat about it was that it was really, truly something different. It really stood out. It really put everybody on its ear. And it was frustrating the shit out of these big companies because they were being propped up by their CD sales, re-releasing.

On my first job at Capital Records, they were just releasing the Beatles on CD. And at the time, that was only 5-7% of sales of CDs. Cassettes were actually a lot more, because people didn't have them in their cars yet. It was a totally different time where it was the changing of the guard. And that's why these indie labels were able to just completely walk in there and take it over. Because they had distribution deals. Priority had it with Capital, Def Jam had it with CBS. That's where the kids would actually find it. But through the distribution in the streets and also through the swapmeets is where they really hit the people who were the early adopters. That and the street promoters getting people to play it on a Saturday night while they were cruising, then at the street merchants they would be able to sell them at a little bit of a discount and just basically get it out there.

JB: Do you remember much about that initial meeting with the band to discuss album cover stuff?

KH: In that case, I believe it was just sitting down in Brian Turner's office, which is the CNN building over there.

JB: On Sunset?

KH: It was at the time, yeah, they still have it. Brian basically knew what he wanted, and that was to get the product out as cheaply as possible. And that's why he loved working with those bands at the time, because the first Ice Cube record sold a million records in ten days and he was laughing like he should have a big cigar in his hand. He had this kind of banker "I can't believe I made all that money today on the stock market" smile. He didn't pay one dime to promote that record and it went platinum. Most of those records were able to promote themselves because there was this groundswell and the kids actually knew how to get it and where to get it. Doug Young, who is the street promoter, was a part of that. And like I said, there was Steve Wills,

Lyrics for the Adults

he is the guy who grew up with N.W.A. and then said, "Wait a minute, the bitches and the hoes thing, I tried to take this home and show my ma!" It's like, I can't believe you're playing that in front of me. So in his family he wasn't able to play it as loud as he would have wished.

But there used to be with these guys a total entourage that would always be in this big huge posse. And truly with DJ Aladdin and Ren and Yella, those guys were really kind of off to the side. They were part of that posse that could still rap, so they were a part of it. There was this group of guys that kind of hooked up and had something in common, and then the barnacles needed to get washed off the bottom of the boat, because they wanted to go a hell of a lot faster. And with these other guys that wanted a percentage of the money, that's why DJ Aladdin, he was erased out of the even *Straight Outta Compton* photographs.

JB: Are you referring to Arabian Prince?

KH: Arabian, I'm sorry, Yeah Arabian Prince.

JB: Yeah, DJ Aladdin was another guy

KH: Yeah, DJ Aladdin was another cover I did. He was a spin master. Yeah, he was with WC.

JB: Yup.

KH: Yeah, WC is actually Ice Cube's cousin.

JB: No kidding? And is that the West side connection?

KH: Yeah, exactly. And if you look in "*AmeriKKKa's Most Wanted*, the front row, you will see a lot of the people you now know and one of them is Dub C. He was also on the cover. Yeah, he was also a little skinny kid.

JB: I'm sure you never realized that kids out in the Midwest like me would be studying these album covers like they were history books or something. Could you talk a little bit about, sounds like at the time there wasn't much, you know it was a job, let's get this done.

KH: Oh yeah, if you looks at the cover of N.W.A., on *Straight Outta Compton*, you turn it over and see who was actually credited as the Art Director, it wasn't me. The reason why its not me is because I wanted 1500 bucks. The girl who did that package, who also went on to Interscope Records and did a lot of stuff, I think she even did *The Chronic*. She was quite successful in that, she got it because she would do the same cover for 1000 bucks and I wanted 1500 bucks. Brian was very cheap and he knew how to make money and he knew how to keep money.

The reason why I knew of Priority Records was Gui Manganiello. Gui was the gentleman who got the "Fuck the Police" FBI letter. He was the one, to my knowledge who actually received that letter. He was also the street promotion guy at Priority Records. He used to work at Capital Records and he said, "Hey there's this cover. I'm at a new company. How would you like to come over and do some work for us?" And I met Brian. It was purely freelance, it was the first freelance stuff that I started doing. Graphic designers tend to be full-time, and every once and a while they might do some freelance, but if the freelance really takes off and they say, "Hey wait a minute, this is really cool, I can wear shorts and a t-shirt to work at home, or work out of my house and I'm in my underwear." The funny part of it is that Brian Turner, Priority Record's first platinum record was, what do you think? The California Raisins.

JB: No way.

KH: You know the California Raisins with "Heard It Through the Grapevine." Yeah, Brian Turner and Mark Surami, who started Priority Records together, and if you look at the Priority Records logo, it's the Porsche logo. He ripped it off.

JB: It is, with the long stretched out type.

KH: Yeah, so if you look at the Priority Records logo, that's how creative Brian was. Creative in the sense that he knew how to make money and he knew how to have somebody else actually do the creative for him, it wasn't important to him.

With the J-cards, you know cassettes, they're called Js because they're the half flap, the spine, and then the panel itself. Most people get four or five panels, so you could get all of the lyrics in there and really show off a lot of the photography you had done. He only wanted to do a J, which was the half flap, which was necessary because the UPC was there, the spine and then the front, the bare, absolute necessary.

JB: I think it was black on the inside.

Lyrics for the Adults

KH: That was it. He didn't want the other ones to flip out because it was too much money. It was a penny per piece, he stated, but it wasn't. It was actually less than that. But he stated, he just sold a million records, a million cassettes, a million records, and he brought me into his office and he said, "You son of a bitch, you used an extra flap. I told you not to use an extra flap, you just wasted me a penny every one of these I sold." He's worried about the 10,000, if it was all cassettes, he's worried about the 10,000 dollars out of the million, whatever that he actually made. He was that way. He knew how to make money and keep it clean. He was a businessman.

So anyway, this other art director did the cover and I did the photoshoot because obviously you had to have the photo first. Brian brought me in, I was working at Capital so I just walked over to the CNN building, which was there at Cahuenga and Sunset, and met Eazy-E. He always wore a baseball cap. He always wore these weird little gloves, like riding gloves, very strange. He always had this little outfit. It was always dark. Everything was dark about him. The Jheri curl was completely pungent. It was at that time the drippy kind of thing, you know, hairstyles were completely different. Right then it was like, "Oh my God, you're such a stereotype." But he played that stereotype, I don't know why, if he felt comfortable in it or if that was actually him trying to push this, "Look I'm a male." Because he had kind of a very high voice, kind of squawky. So Brian and he and I were just talking about doing the cover and none of them really gave a crap about it, like I said. "We need an image, you know a photographer." And I said, "Yeah, I know one from school." Eric Poppelton was my friend from school. He was the only photographer at the time that I knew. I was like "Yeah, I know this guy." "Ok great, he better be cheap. I don't want to spend any money. And if we can get him for that, we need to do Eazy's cover also. *Eazy-Duz-It*. And maybe we can just do it the same day."

And then I convinced them that if you wanted to do a day shot/night shot kind of thing, it will have to be two separate days. But we didn't have any decent photography equipment at the time. I mean, usually you can spend thousands of dollars, not only on the room, the space that you're going to have, or locations and props and all that, but also the lighting packages. You can easily spend several thousand on a lighting package. We had a strobe, and the skull-

Lyrics for the Adults

and-crossbones was basically just a little image that I found, I think from a library. And we just projected it up on the overpass. So it was like, we had no money. And we weren't spending any money so it was like, "Uh, I don't know. They're like bad motherfuckers. Let's put a skull and cross bones up there." It's like "that's so pirate." What were we thinking? But they didn't care. They were just excited that they would get their photograph taken. They would always come in this huge group. You know, like how many cars did they come in?

Do you remember Coolio?

JB: Oh yeah.

KH: Coolio would come into Priority Records and he had just gotten a girl pregnant and he was the caretaker. He was daddy daycare. And here was Coolio, you know, I know him from just being a young dad, and he would have his kid in one hand and his cassette in the other and he was just going up to Priority whenever those guys would come up, he was like, "Hey, can I come with you?" And he'd basically kind of hang out and try to talk to everybody. And that was the other thing, I always wondered if it was like Detroit. If it was ever that way with Motown, where people would just come in, in a convoy and try to get somebody's attention to sign them. But Coolio, I remember him just changing diapers in my office. And then he never got signed by Priority. He had to go somewhere else.

A funny thing about MC Hammer, it was just him and his brother. And we looked at the artwork on the floor and we picked the cover shots. The second time I was already at Priority Records, so I didn't do his second or his third. But I was told that there was a big, huge stretch limo because he had made it with "Let's get it Started". It did really well, two million I think. And he came with a stretch limo and he had all these people, you know, like a clown car, with dancers and everybody just trying to get signed. And he was trying to sign everybody and get them these deals. His next album, the third album there, I was told that he came with two stretch limos and even more people jumped out trying to get their contracts signed. By the time I did him again at Giant Records, he was canned off of Capital, he was driving himself again. So, this too shall pass. Because all of those guys are basically the same way. They would all run in as a pack, everyone of them were all kind of working on their own little solo projects.

For the cover of "Niggaz4Life," where they're kind of floating up like ghosts, to show the whole N.W.A. crew the cover, I went over to one of the houses that Eazy-E had. He was a very good businessman. He actually had several houses in Compton. He was really an entrepreneur. I went over to his house to show them the cover because it would actually have to be photo-retouched and a composite because they were kind of floating out of their bodies. It was like mom-and-dad-weren't-home kind of house. It was just a bunch of stinky, twenty-five year old guys, watching cartoons, eating Doritos. Seriously it was the funniest scene. It was like, "Guys, you gotta get a job." But it was like, they were selling millions of records, they don't need to get a job. But I was like "You're 18, if I was your dad I'd say, 'Get a job.'" Anyway, we showed them the cover and they were really interested in it, and for some reason I had some stuff of Ice Cube's, too. And they were very jealous when Ice Cube left, full of animosity. You can hear it in some of the lyrics, back-and-forth. There was a big back-and-forth vibe at the time it was also with the Tupac and Biggie stuff. There was this whole death thing and threats and East coast and West Coast, like warring tribes. So what do you guys do? It's like you're basically in the recording studios, you're at home eating Doritos, or you're at the clubs. And its like, "How do you get into these huge tiffs?"

JB: Did they want to see Ice Cube's artwork?

KH: Yeah, they actually wanted to see it. I probably brought it by just to piss them off or at least see what they'd think. For some reason I had it and they were really skeptical and interested and it was like, "What's that about, what's this, what's that? What do you call the cover?" But it was funny how it was kind of the scorned kind of friendship thing. You left, they knew that he was a huge talent because he was writing most of the their songs, and they really had an issue with it. The "Hundred Miles and Runnin" was, I think, probably one of their best songs and it was after Ice Cube had left.

JB: It was artistically drawn.

KH: Yeah, it was a painting. The sad thing about that thing is that to have scale, it's a hundred miles and running, they basically just broke out of jail.

JB: Right.

KH: They wanted it so it was like a painting. You know, like a bad Corman kind of film. Basically if you're going to have four people running, escaping, you're not going to have them all jogging exactly across like they're doing craftwork on stage right where they're just these heads and they're all the same size. You want somebody in the foreground, you want someone who's just fallen and needs to get up, and the other guy looking behind his back.

JB: You can only see like half of Eazy's face right up in the foreground.

KH: And the whole thing was, because of Brian being kind of cost-prudent, it was done for the cassette. The cassette has to be like this so everyone was like, "Why is Eazy's face so big? This is bullshit." And I was like, "No, we had to do it for the cassette and the album." So he's only supposed to be like his eyeball and this for the cassette, because it was mostly cassettes that they sold more than albums. But the one that everyone remembers and also the platinum record that came out, Eazy-E's head is this big and everybody else's stupid and insignificant. And there was always a rivalry with Eazy since he was the power behind that group. He worked tight with Jerry Heller, doing their mischief. It felt like there was a little bit of distrust because they didn't really know if they were going to be in the band next year or not. So, they were really a kind of just playing to make sure that they were cool. And they were all doing other side-projects too.

JB: When was the first time that you realized that you had been a part of a major phenomenon? Do you remember a time that it kind of hit you?

KH: When I realized that was a pretty huge album?

JB: Yeah, when you realized you were part of a pretty huge cultural phenomenon there.

KH: When I could get work just by saying I did it. Everything in this portfolio at one time here was just all black bands. Mike Concepcion, he founded the Crips or the Bloods, one of them. He's in a wheelchair.

JB: He did the "We're All in the Same Gang" project and record with N.W.A. Mike Concepcion.

KH: Yeah, Mike Concepcion. So, Kevin is kind of a black name. Ha ha. A lot of guys I know that are Kevin, which is my name, happen to be black. Like

Lyrics for the Adults

I said, I could get any work in that industry at that time. In *Rap Pages* there were 25, if there were 50 images in that piece and 18 of them were mine. I also did the first Lexus site, I designed the first Lexus site. And that's because I was really into what's new. I always knew what was new.

You asked "Did you know that you were going to see something out of this or were you just doing a project?" I thought it was fun because you'd never heard it before and you couldn't show it to your mom kind of thing. And it wasn't something that you shouldn't actually be proud of because it was so street. It didn't have the credit that a large label would. I mean the same year I did John Lennon's *Imagine*, the soundtrack to the film. That's the stuff that you put in your portfolio. Those guys could care F-ing less about any of that stuff. It was, "You did *Compton*?" Yeah, it was because I could get a job. Mike Concepcion—so I was dropping off this portfolio and again there were a bunch of guys, they were always in packs, always with their homies. I walk through the door and I said, "Hey I'm Kevin and I'm here to talk to somebody about a cover." And they just started busting up laughing and Mike Concepcion said, "I'm sorry what did you say your name was, David Duke?" That was down at the time when David Duke was popular and I was like, "Dude, don't dis me like that. That's complete crap. I'm just here to help you out." And I actually kind of held my own a little bit when these people were as important as they were. Mike Concepcion with his affiliations and all of these guys. But if you hold your own, they respect you a hell of a lot more.

When I was working with the Beastie Boys, Adam Yauch was completely pixel-pushing me to move shit around and finally I just said, "Fuck you. No, how about you fuck yourself." And, well, you don't say that. You get fired for that kind of thing, and I said, "Go fuck yourself, I can't work with you anymore, because you gotta let me do this and stop micromanaging me." Because they were complete jerks. They were spray painting graffiti all over Capital Records. They didn't do well through promotion on that cover because they were kind of assholes to all the crew coming out. They were Def Jam and then they came out to Capital. They were complete assholes. Arrogant assholes. And they had every right to be. But I just had enough of it, and I had a bad day and I couldn't do it but like an hour later, he comes back into my office, Yauch, and was like, "Dude, I'm so sorry." And then we were best friends and everything was cool.

Lyrics for the Adults

So Mike Concepcion, he kept calling me David Duke in this meeting, so I leave after showing them this stuff, and like I said, I could get a job by that one album, and all the other stuff, like doing Tupac's first also. These guys gave me that credibility but they all thought it was a black guy doing that stuff. But with that cover, I was called by the AR Director later, the project manager, and he says, "Yeah, you weren't dark enough." And I said, "That's total crap. You saw my package portfolio right? I've done everything out there." Everything out there that is the stuff that everyone's emulating is the stuff that I've done. He was like, "Well they want somebody else." So there was a lot of strange, reverse racism.

They were all paranoid. When we did *Niggaz4Life*, they hung out in the van while the shot was being set up and being photographed. They would only come out to take their shot and then they were gone because they were targets. One of the things you asked about the first meetings, one of the things I also asked was red or blue? What can't I use? Red or blue? Bloods and the Crips. N.W.A. was red and you'll never see blue on those covers. But it was all gang affiliation and it was very strange to work in that little world. That was a starter gun, by the way [pointing to N.W.A. album].

JB: Did you bring the gun to the shoot?

KH: No, he [Eazy-E] had it. And I think it was just for him to do this kind of thing. I don't know if he thought he was going to photograph it that way when he brought it, but he said it was a starter gun. But as we slowly got further and further into a lot of these other things, it got more intense. Like I did OFTB, Operation From the Bottom. Those guys were completely from the projects and that's what the interesting thing here is, they spurred on this, like an Obama kind of thing. If they can do it, I can do it. Oh my god, cause I've got something to look forward to, cause I'm a skinny kid who's not as tall as I need to be for basketball and I'm not big enough to play football. I got that and I can do some rhymes. So they completely gave people hope. Kids thought in their heads that they could absolutely do it. And what was weird is that in a strange, sad way, for the West coast stuff, it was about not gang affiliation, but a kind of gang kind innuendo and ambience.

Lyrics for the Adults

So, street credibility was a gang affiliation. And they were just kind of putting on a play, or at least that's what I thought it was. Look through *The Source* magazine for fifteen years. You'll see the same thing. It went South and then there was a certain point where it realized that it had to be hip-hop or it wouldn't get anywhere. And it was the West coast, East coast kind of thing. And they were getting radio play because they realized that was kind of whack and it was passé. And they needed to go onto something else because they were now getting radio play. Where this opened the box, now they had the door open, and now they wanted to make money. So they actually shifted because of the money issue, and it was getting played.

JB: You did *Death Certificate*?

KH: Yeah, the funny thing about *Death Certificate* is the handwriting right there, two things. He wasn't there the day that we shot that, it was his soon-to-be-wife's birthday, and he completely spaced. It was like 5,000 dollars, which was a lot of money for Brian Turner. So we had this old guy on a gurney—this was Ice Cube's idea. And he was basically in this old psycho-ward, but what was pathetic about it was that he wasn't there for the photo shoot and we spent $5,000 or something to drop him in before Photoshop. To just drop him into it, and Brian Turner who was such a cheap guy, said "You can't even tell that he wasn't there, why did I spend all that money.?" I said, "Exactly! It looks as if he was there." And we lit it again the same way. What was kind of funny was that the handwriting on this Uncle Sam was actually my dad's. He was painting the eaves of my house, he came out from Texas to help paint my house, and I said, "Hey dad, write Uncle Sam on this." So he wrote it and I dropped it on the scanner, so that's my dad's handwriting, but he wrote it on the roof of my house.

The other one with this [*Death Certificate*] is, its actually a real gun. Because with the blanks, if its not a real, if it's a starter gun, or if its kind of a fake one, it has a red plug in it. So for hand props you actually have to sign it out properly, its actually kind of strange. So anyway you can't have a felony and all of that kind of thing, so the idea was that when we were shooting this, and it was pretty much playing directly off of this guy. [pointing to N.W.A. album] And actually Eric has a starter gun in his hand, that's not a real gun.

JB: Is that right?

KH: Yeah, it's just a starter gun. It's a skinny one. But with this, instead of having it so he was basically shooting at you, or any of that kind of stuff, because we had already done that, you got so much confidence saying, how about if its you handing that person the gun saying "You have absolutely no balls to be able to do it." So the look on his face is like, go ahead, *Kill at Will*. Instead of him doing that, which was offensive, a black man with a gun.

JB: Right. Interesting. Street Knowledge Records?

KH: That's right. With Pat Charbonnet. Yeah, Pat Charbonnet was the publicist for Priority Records. And she was the one who realized that Ice Cube was not at the point that he should be in his career. I think the reason why is that he was making 500 extra for writing all of those songs on the record, and he felt as if he was being completely abused. And Pat Charbonnet, as the story goes, that means we're just talking, that she convinced him that he was much more than just a player for Eric and all of these other guys. She told Cube, "You're the success of this, you're the person who should be out there a lot more."

JB: You did Tupac's first album?

KH: Yeah, that was the other funny thing. When I was doing Tupac, he came down from San Francisco, that "Do what you like"-

JB: Digital Underground.

KH: He was in Digital Underground. He came down and was at the Burbank airport across the street. And I had never seen anyone with that much bling on before, and his girlfriend was completely decked out also, and here he just came down for a quick dialogue on the cover and stuff like that. I walk into the bathroom, excuse myself to go to the bathroom and he comes in right behind me and goes, "That's where I've seen you before." And I was at the urinal and I thought it was kind of inappropriate and an odd statement. And he goes no, no, no, it was N.W.A., you were in that cover weren't you. And he remembered the back of my head from that cover.

JB: That's you? No way.

KH: Yeah, the reason why I'm in that shot, because my daughter, who was the little white girl eating watermelon, which was the complete role reversal, was that she was only one and a half. She's now graduated from UCSD cum laude in anthropology, she's one of four of my children. She was completely petrified of the guys, cause there are like nine, big guys there. So she was kind of intimidated. So I said, "How about if I'm shining their shoes?" It's obviously white tennis shoes, so it doesn't have any sense to it, but the fact was that here these guys are being waited on, and the white girl is not the black baby that's dirty and barefoot, but it's the role reversal of "we're now on top and we have something to say." And that's what that whole thing was. And that was the one shot that was in competition for the front of *Straight Outta Compton*. We shot it the same day. The debate was, what's going to get the most impact, and Brian Turner really knew controversy. And he really was thinking, "That doesn't say as much, and its not as good of a shot of these people." That other photo gives that sense of "Who the hell are these people?"

The day we did the photo shoot, we did that downtown, in little Tokyo, that was the only alleys that I knew of. I was like, "Hey let's go down and take some alley shots." But the idea that was presented to them was the first one with the little white girl eating watermelon and they just thought that was the craziest thing they had ever heard and they were just laughing at me like, "Why would you be doing that? Why would you put your kid into that position?" That was my first daughter. With my last daughter, I proposed to Ice Cube when we were shooting the *Kill at Will* shot, that just like Grace Jones' famous shot of her holding her baby upside down naked, I was thinking, "How would you like to hold a little white girl upside down, what do you think about that? It's kind of like the Beatles and *Meet the Beatles* where all of the meat is all over them and the baby parts and stuff like that? You want to go that far?" And he goes, "You're a crazy motherfucker, no way! I'll just do the gun. Give me the gun." And so he did the gun instead.

JB: That's hilarious.

Lyrics for the Adults

Interview with The D.O.C.

John Bucher: I'm sure you've been asked a lot about how you connected with N.W.A., so most of the stuff we want to talk about today is about your involvement with the making of *Straight Outta Compton* and then about the making of your album, *No One Can Do It Better*.

Doc: Fire Away.

JB: There's been quite a bit of discussion about your involvement in the writing of *Straight Outta Compton*. Can you talk to us a bit about the how the process for creating the album went? I've heard that you were really responsible for all of Eazy-E's lyrics and anything that Dre rapped. Tell us a bit about what the process was for creating the songs on the album.

Doc: I like to tell people that making a great album is like knocking somebody the fuck out. You can't do it with one finger. It takes five fingers balled up together and clenched in a fist to knock somebody on they ass. And no matter who was individually responsible for any particular thing, we were all involved in every aspect of everything as far as that album was concerned. With the exception of Eazy on the mic, more like he was the inspiration behind a lot of stuff, you know?

JB: Right.

Doc: He didn't do a lot of the work physically, but he was the inspiration behind a lot of the work.

JB: Very cool.

Doc: It is true that I wrote a lot of his stuff and quite a bit of Dre's stuff, but I'm no gangsta per se. And I say that because, number one, I'm from West Dallas, Texas, where they hadn't even heard of gang banging yet. So it was all relatively new to me. For me, it was just about finding a way to make Eazy-E as interesting as Ice Cube with the difference in dynamics of their performing abilities. And with the fact that Eazy's rhythm was almost non-existent, we had to really work around his persona. For me it was about making him more funny and to take the edge off of how gritty the other guys' performances were.

Lyrics for the Adults

JB: Would it be fair to say that you really helped to create this character that Eazy-E became?

Doc: I'd say that's a fair assessment sure, but like I said, we all did this together, there were many times in the studio where I would write something for Eazy, or even for myself or Dre or anybody, and then I'd come in and hear what Cube wrote and say, "Well, fuck that." And I'd take my shit home and redo my shit. I can't let the guy do me like that. And there were times when I'd come in and Cube would hear my stuff and be like "Fuck that!" And I'd go home and rewrite my stuff and it was a family. And during those first few years that's really what it was. We were, before the money came, we were really a family.

JB: I want to talk specifically about the song "Parental Discretion iz Advised" because that's obviously one song where you not only contribute lyrics but you're the head lyricist on that song. Can you talk a little bit about how that particular song came about?

Doc: It's kind of funny because the other guys in N.W.A., they didn't really want me on their stuff, you know, I didn't get a chance to showcase on a lot of other songs. Because they really made it a point to make sure that I knew that I wasn't really a part of the group. Like I said, I was just the new dude from Texas and I just happened to be real good, but I wasn't straight outta Compton. And that really pissed me off in the early days, because when they took pictures, I had to stand off on the side and watch and it really started to hurt my feelings. I understood what they were saying, I just didn't really agree with how they were saying it, but with "Parental Discretion," I really wanted to tear they ass up. That was my mindset. I really wanted to dig in they ass on that record. And I really wanted to show America that I was a badass. And then, I had a huge ego and probably still got it. But you know, I was straight outta Texas.

JB: Well, it's certainly not the only time on the record that we hear your voice. The song "Fuck the Police" is probably the best known song off the album and obviously we hear you on that song kind of playing the part of the court bailiff. Can you talk a little bit about your involvement with that song and again coming from Dallas you probably had a different perspective but you probably were aware of the issues between the police department and young black men.

Lyrics for the Adults

Doc: I'll tell you something again. There is not a corner on this green globe that somebody doesn't think to themselves every day "Fuck the Police." We will be driving down the street, get pulled over by any kind of police and they'll talk shit to you because they have the power to do it. And it doesn't matter if you're right or wrong, it's just the human part of them that wants to fuck with you, and there ain't shit you can do. And that's really how that song came about, because one morning me and Dre were trying to rush to the studio and got pulled over and they gave the guy a huge ticket, and I think that where that song really came from.

Like I said, I don't think that there's a corner on the globe where somebody at some point ain't telling the police, "Fuck you!" Now I'm clean as a whistle, I haven't had any problems with them motherfuckers in years, but every time one of them gets behind me in my car, I get that funny feeling in my stomach, like "Oh shit." But at the same time, as a grown man, I do recognize and realize how vitally important police in this country are. It kind of stinks that society as a whole doesn't understand that even though these people have badges on, underneath those black uniforms they are still human beings. And human beings can be full of shit.

JB: One of the things that has been said a lot about that song, and this kind of connects to who you are as an artist, is that it wasn't just a rant, there was a lot of intelligence behind the song, and the topic was discussed with a lot of intelligence. You have been described by people who are familiar with your music as someone with a lot of intelligence behind your music. You've mentioned in the past that books have been an important part of your life, but can you talk a little bit about the depth of your lyrical writing and how that has been influential even in the work that you did with N.W.A.?

Doc: I like to think of myself as an intelligent man, as a thinking person. I don't do things just for the sake of doing, though I don't judge those who seemingly do so, because music is not to be judged, it's to be loved. If there's one song you don't like, then change the CD. It's your prerogative. I would consider myself a writer more than a rapper. It means more to me to teach than it does to motivate you to shake your ass. If I can do both at the same time, that's pretty cool. But when I got my record, you'll notice that there's not a lot of anger, there's not a lot of murder, death, killing. The one thing I really talked about on that album is me, because that's really all I knew a whole lot about at that particular point in time in my life. But as an MC, I modeled myself after who I thought was the best MC in the whole wide world at the time: Rakim. And I wanted to be better than Rakim. If I could be better than Rakim, then I would have reached my goal in life. And I can recall people making that comparison over the years, and I thought to myself that Rakim had three or four albums and I only got to do one, which makes me believe that I must have reached my goal. And the people know it.

JB: Absolutely. I hear that comparison a lot, even though you're from Dallas, as far as the West coast goes, I know for a long time people dubbed you the West coast Rakim. So that definitely is true to form.

Can you tell us a little bit about the process of making *Straight Outta Compton*? Any other stories from the studio?

Doc: I'll give you a few little things about those days that were cool.

Dr. Dre was the most incredible human being I had ever met. And I sat there and listened to him like a fucking puppy, just to watch him, even though I couldn't figure out what he's doing. I just liked to watch the dude do the shit. You know, because like directors make movies, he was always able to see the end of the song before we started it. That's why all these songs usually have a visual in them, when you play his music, or at least in those days, you could see, you could see the shit, while the song played, and it motivated you like it was a scene in a movie or something. Dre had the ability to do that before he started making the beat and he would tell you the scene and you could fix it in your mind and then you could create the words around that picture. That just fucking blew my mind about this guy and I always knew, since 1988 when I met him, that he was the music while I was the words. And if I stayed close to him, I could be great.

Ice Cube was probably the strongest in the group personality-wise. He didn't take shit, but talking to everybody. He came in would fuck with Eazy all day long. He would bag on Eric's laugh all day long and I thought that was cool because nobody else did that. You know Eazy was sort of the man and Ren was Eazy's sidekick so you never saw one without the other one. He was kind of a weird guy. He didn't hang around all the time. He was always off on his own shit. And he was just a weird dude to me. What did I leave out?

JB: I guess Arabian Prince was only around for a minute, right?

Doc: No, no Arabian Prince was gone before I got there. But Eazy, who didn't know shit about music, who didn't know shit about rapping, he would spend most of the time he was there arguing with Dre about what the fuck Dre should do. And it would really piss Dre off. So much to the point that Dre would just shut the shit down and we'd all leave. Because Eazy was in there fucking with him all the time. I thought that was funny as hell. Eazy stayed at the piano even though he could never play a lick, but the one thing that I really respected about Eric was, even though he didn't have the talent, he worked harder than anybody to get the shit right. It was natural for me. I would go in there and they used to call me "one take Willy." Because songs like "The Formula" and "Fuck the Police" you know I did those in one take. It didn't take me long at all, as a matter of fact, *No One Could Do It Better* we did that album in three weeks. We did the album in three weeks and there are no extra songs. Every song you heard is the song as we did it.

JB: Can you talk a little bit about Eazy's solo album, which a lot of people consider N.W.A.'s first album. Were you around for that and what do you remember about that project in those days?

Doc: The first day that I went to the studio with Dre. The first day he came and picked me up in Compton. I was standing by this high school called Centennial in an all-Blood neighborhood. I didn't know shit about Bloods and Crips and all that shit until I came outside and went up the street trying to get me some chicken, which is a pretty interesting story, I'll tell you later. But Dre told me, he came and got me and took me to the studio. And he had this drum playing, and I met all the guys who, it was my first time meeting them. And Dre asked me, "Can you put some words to this beat?" And I said, "Hell yeah." And it took me about fifteen minutes and I went in there and laid the song and that song would become "We Want Eazy." And that was the first song I ever did in this group. And I did it on the first day I got to the studio. And it took all of about twenty minutes to do the song. That's how I used to do it back then, man, I was firing 'em out back then.

Lyrics for the Adults

JB: Let's talk for a second about one of the songs off your album—"The Grand Finale." I always remember hearing that song and thinking, "Man, it sounds like this is all live musicians," and it's the last song that the original lineup of N.W.A. was on. It's the last song that Ice Cube was on as a part of N.W.A.. Can you talk a little bit about "The Grand Finale?"

Doc: "The Grand Finale" in so many different ways is such a poetic record. Because that's exactly what it was—it was the last song that we would all do together. And who knows, God works in strange ways.

JB: Indeed.

Doc: But it was the last song that we would all be on together. And it was the last song on our record, it was a way for us to be done, get the fuck out. We're done, we're finished. Let's move on to the next topic, next subject. Those guys were touring back then, so Dre didn't have a lot of time to work on my record. But that particular track was all Dre. And like I told you before, he came in, he had the idea already in his head, he told us all what it was, and then he made it. He made the beat. Well, actually, he played the drums and the musicians played all the tracks, so that shit—it was a fun record. There was really no hard work involved in that one.

JB: Again, it was Ice Cube's last time out with N.W.A.. Can you talk for a bit about your relationship with Ice Cube? It sounds like you guys really challenged each other—especially in N.W.A. projects, to constantly make better music.

Doc: I respect Ice Cube, in my humble opinion. He's the heart and soul of N.W.A. He was the reason N.W.A. worked. He was the essence of what that whole thing was about, to me. He was the strongest lyricist, or MC on the West coast during that time, besides myself. His words were that strong and powerful. And the way he connected words, the way he connected them so simply and in such an everyday conversational way. You know, simplicity is the sincerest form of genius.

I wanted to be as good as him all the time. So that should show how I respected him. On a more personal note, Ice Cube is a good dude. And he continues to be a good friend to this day. If I called him and I needed him, even though he's a million-dollar movie-making man now, he'd come. And that says

Lyrics for the Adults

more about the character of the man than any song you can make. And when its all said and done, you can make a thousand motherfucking records, and you can make a billion motherfucking dollars, but if your character is short, you'll end up with squat. In my opinion, that's why Suge Knight had so many issues, because his character was not that strong. He had it all in his hands, and now it seems like every time you pick up a newspaper, somebody's beating the guy up.

JB: Can we talk about looking back on the entire album, *Straight Outta Compton*? Now its 20 years later, we've got some history behind us. Can you talk about the importance of that record and just why 20 years later we're still talking about *Straight Outta Compton*?

Doc: I will give you the exact reason why that record is so important. Because it spawned two decades of rap music. Its like rap music got to that point, after 1988, '89, and *Straight Outta Compton* came out, and every rap record of any major consequence since then is that record. Everybody, nobody is making, even if you want to refer to this shit as gangsta shit. Nobody saw the need to take it any further than that. Everybody that's rappin' is a dope dealer who will kill you. It has not changed since fuckin' 1988. That is the M.O. If you are a dope dealer who will kill someone, then you too can be rich and wealthy rappin'. It's like that's the mantra. And I don't judge that. It is what it is. Now I said at one point in the game, you want to blame gangsta rap for the effects that its had? That's like trying to charge dope, its like trying to charge the drugs for distribution instead of the dealer. You can't blame the product without blaming the guy with the product in his hand, and I don't mean the people making the music. Like you don't blame the Colombians, you blame the niggas on the corner selling the dope. You have to use that same strategy, that same frame of mind when it comes to records that people buy in stores, because drugs, sex, money, and murder sells. Always has, always will. But if that's the only thing that the powers that be are shoving, then that's the only thing that people are gonna be accepting. And that just is what it is. And I don't hate that because this is a capitalist society, and make your money. That's why I'm so excited that I'll be able to have another opportunity to make another record with my voice, or a voice strong enough that I can get my point across because I'm talking shit to everybody. I mean you can make a list of every motherfucking body that has anything to do with record-making or selling, and I'm talking shit about every last one of them motherfuckers. I mean I'm even talking shit to myself on that damn record.

JB: You touched on it, but can you speak a bit about where you wanna go, where you see things going for the Doc?

Doc: Well, I'm like Dr. Dre right now. I wanna make one more record. And I've been blessed. G-O-D has blessed me to get a voice back. To get a voice back. And its not the same, but at least 70% of what I had, I can have again. And that's all I need, goddammit. And a lot of motherfuckers are in trouble, because I can sing some Pavarotti shit on your ass with 70% of what I had. Make it sound so good that a twelve-year-old girl will laugh at you. And I'm fucking dead serious. I mean that with every piece of fucking spermicidal juice I got in my balls I mean that. But it's not really about me any more. It's bigger than the D.O.C. The D.O.C. is pretty insignificant in the whole scheme of things. It is a testimony to faith and determination and pride and never giving up. In my opinion, the record is more about hip-hop than it is about me, or at least what hip-hop stood for when I loved it.

JB: That then, you got me excited. I cannot wait to see what you do, we just really love your music.

Doc: Hey bro, I really appreciate that, it means a lot. I don't take any of it for granted. I've learned my lesson. I did at one point take that shit for granted, but I don't anymore. I understand that it's a blessing. It's not a privilege. For a motherfucker to get up in front of 20,000 and be able to do this shit. It's not a right, it's a privilege and a blessing. And I don't hate any of these young guys, from MC Hammer's old ass to the young guys in Dallas doing the stankylegs, all of that. I love it all. If you are African American or any other minority or even a white boy, I love shady, in this business, and you can make money, then God bless you kid, go get that money. Because there are a zillion and one things worse that you could be doing.

www.ingramcontent.com/pod-product-compliance
Lightning Source LLC
LaVergne TN
LVHW090116080426
835507LV00040B/917